YORK NOTES

Cat's Eye

Margaret Atwood

Note by Madeleine MacMurraugh-Kavanagh

 Longman   York Press

ACKNOWLEDGEMENT

The author wishes to thank Margaret Atwood for permission to quote from *Cat's Eye*, and also the publisher Virago for permission to reproduce extracts from *Conversations*, Earl G. Ingersoll, ed., Margaret Atwood
© O.W. Toad Ltd, 1988

Madeleine MacMurraugh-Kavanagh is hereby identified as author of this work in accordance with Section 77 of the Copyright, Designs and Patents Act 1988

YORK PRESS
322 Old Brompton Road, London SW5 9JH

PEARSON EDUCATION LIMITED
Edinburgh Gate, Harlow,
Essex CM20 2JE, United Kingdom
Associated companies, branches and representatives throughout the world

First published 2000

ISBN 0–582–42479–8

Designed by Vicki Pacey
Phototypeset by Gem Graphics, Trenance, Mawgan Porth, Cornwall
Colour reproduction and film output by Spectrum Colour
Produced by Addison Wesley Longman China Limited, Hong Kong

C ONTENTS

PART ONE

INTRODUCTION

HOW TO STUDY A NOVEL

Studying a novel on your own requires self-discipline and a carefully thought-out work plan in order to be effective.

- You will need to read the novel more than once. Start by reading it quickly for pleasure, then read it slowly and thoroughly.

- On your second reading make detailed notes on the plot, characters and themes of the novel. Further readings will generate new ideas and help you to memorise the details of the story.

- Some of the characters will develop as the plot unfolds. How do your responses towards them change during the course of the novel?

- Think about how the novel is narrated. From whose point of view are events described?

- A novel may or may not present events chronologically: the time-scheme may be a key to its structure and organisation.

- What part do the settings play in the novel?

- Are words, images or incidents repeated so as to give the work a pattern? Do such patterns help you to understand the novel's themes?

- Identify what styles of language are used in the novel.

- What is the effect of the novel's ending? Is the action completed and closed, or left incomplete and open?

- Does the novel present a moral and just world?

- Cite exact sources for all quotations, whether from the text itself or from critical commentaries. Wherever possible find your own examples from the novel to back up your opinions.

- Always express your ideas in your own words.

This York Note offers an introduction to *Cat's Eye* and cannot substitute for close reading of the text and the study of secondary sources.

Cat's Eye is a novel about the savage world of little girls. In the story of Elaine Risley, the reader finds a harrowing record of victimisation, shame and denial. What results is an account of physical and psychic survival, and an analysis of the shattering long-term consequences of childhood brutality.

Cat's Eye is a *Künstlerroman*, a novel that focuses on the development of an artist. It is a **fictive autobiography** that constructs a fictional life-story in tracing the history and experiences of an invented middle-aged painter, Elaine Risley. Though Margaret Atwood distances herself from her protagonist (she has repeatedly become irritated when interviewers confuse her with her characters), there is a significant degree of overlap between the novelist's life-story and that of her fictional character. Atwood's father was an entomologist and, like Elaine Risley, the novelist's early childhood was spent accompanying her family on field trips to the wilderness spaces of Northern Canada. Further similarities between the novelist's life-story and that of her fictional protagonist are outlined by Atwood in the following interview: 'I did not attend a full year of school until I was in grade eight ... I began writing at the age of five, but there was a dark period between the ages of eight and sixteen when I didn't write. I started again at sixteen and have no idea why, but it was suddenly the only thing I wanted to do' (Margaret Atwood, *Conversations*, p. 70).

If 'writing' is substituted for 'painting', this account strongly resembles the fictional life-story of Elaine Risley. Is *Cat's Eye*, then, fictive autobiography or autobiographical fiction? The division between the two is certainly confusing, but it seems clear that the novelist is simply drawing from her own experience in supplying material information about her characters. This does not mean that the traumas suffered by Elaine in *Cat's Eye* have been suffered by Atwood herself. The 'life-story' that the novelist creates for her protagonist is an account of a fictional life and it thus constitutes a fictive autobiography.

The first-person mode in which the novel is written creates a sense of intimacy between the narrator and the reader. The details of Elaine's life are provided through a patchwork of intersecting narratives, as the painter reconstructs the events of her past through her artworks and dreams, and through her memories. These memories have been repressed by her for most of her adult life, but her paintings and dreams have become a repository for the terror, pain and hatred that scar her psyche as a result of the two-year trauma she suffered as a child. As such, the paintings are ciphers that require decoding by the reader. They are **allegorical** representations that explain the riddle of Elaine's 'lost' years, and Elaine is as blind to their coded meanings as the reader is until the events of her childhood are reenacted in the narrative. A constant movement results between the coded story of the artworks and dreams (the **figural** narrative) and the reenacted (narrated) story of Elaine's trauma (the **discursive** narrative). Both forms of narrative produce autobiographical 'versions' and 'sub-versions' of a life: held in tension with each other, the two personal 'testimonies' combine to produce the complete life-story of Elaine Risley.

As Elaine wanders around contemporary Toronto, the site of her childhood terror, memories are triggered which produce a constant movement between the past and the present tense. *Cat's Eye* is a 'retrospective' at every level of narrative and of meaning. The term is initially used to refer to Elaine's 'retrospective' exhibition of paintings, the event for which she has been persuaded to return to Toronto. However, as the novel develops, and as the movement between past and present is initiated, it becomes clear that *Cat's Eye* involves a 'retrospective' of Elaine's life. The discourses upon time (or, more accurately, space-time) that echo throughout the text further alert the reader to the fact that 'time' is here perceived in terms that deny our familiar experience of linear flow from past, through present, and towards the future. Instead, time is here regarded as a series of stacked levels. As such, Elaine is painfully aware that she is living her 'past' in her 'present' so that the two are seen to coexist. After all, as Atwood insists at a crucial point, 'Nothing goes away' (p. 3).

It is therefore too much to hope that Elaine's 'future' can be anything other than fundamentally compromised from the outset. However, at the end of the novel, hope is suggested in the open-ended conclusion to Elaine's story which implies a hesitant faith in survival (a key term in Canadian literature). *Cat's Eye* is not 'closed down' at the end of the narrative because this would be to deny the ongoing nature of Elaine's struggle, but even if the future is uncertain for Elaine, a future tense is at least seen to be possible for her where once it had not appeared to be so.

Readers are initially swept along by *Cat's Eye* at the level of its story-line. The 'read-on-ness' created by Atwood in this largely 'inner space', introspective novel is partly a result of narrative pace. While the present-tense Toronto narratives which open each section move at a leisurely speed, the 'retrospective' visits to Elaine's childhood gallop through the years. The reader is also gripped by the several layers of action and observation that complement and contextualise Elaine's life-story. The social documentary relating to the past and present of Toronto contextualises Elaine's 'inner space' story in an 'outer space' world of socio-political event, sight and sound. In addition, Elaine's life is littered with problematic relationships (particularly with other women), so that hers is by no means an underpopulated world. And always, of course, there lurks the sinister presence/absence of Cordelia, one of the most enigmatic and intriguing characters ever to have appeared in Margaret Atwood's fiction.

Though Elaine seems an isolated and shadowy figure, her wry appraisals of those around her provide another level of interest to the story. Indeed, the narrator's humour balances her evident pain, and her consistently **ironic** tone, her sometimes ruthless self-mockery, and her talent for **parody** produce a narrative voice that is human and engaged. Further, both Elaine's 'inner' and 'outer' spaces are detailed with an attention to colour, smell, texture and shape that betrays a painter's 'eye'. This attention to visceral experience is another outstanding characteristic of the novel, particularly as 'sight' is connected to a chain of images and **metaphors** that combine to create an unmistakable focus upon vision. Margaret Atwood uses the notion of 'vision' in surprising ways so that a complex network of meanings results. These meanings are vital to the narrative method and metaphorical patterns in this novel.

Despite the apparent difficulty of several of the intellectual discourses and theories circulating in *Cat's Eye* (astrophysics is the most obvious, but no discourse is prioritised over the others), the novel is fully accessible to readers with little or no knowledge of these fields. However, a full appreciation of Atwood's use of metaphor, as well as an understanding of her narrative strategies and of her methods of creating meaning, can only be achieved if some familiarity with these theoretical areas is attained.

Since *Cat's Eye* is a multi-levelled novel making use of several interweaving discourses and narrative strategies, how should readers approach the text? The novel should initially be read 'to see what happens': as the story is digested, the reader will automatically note key themes and images which structure the text. Central narrative devices will also emerge from a first reading. At the same time, certain questions should be considered. For example, how is Elaine's life-story 'written' in different versions? How do the accounts of this story differ according to the 'angle of vision' from which they are viewed? How are different **discourses** fused together, and how do they connect with each other to provide a unified network of meaning?

Second and third read-throughs of the novel, together with exercises in close textual analysis, will lead to an increasingly clear understanding of the devices Atwood uses.

In Elaine Risley's story of trauma, repression and resistance, the reader encounters a narrative that celebrates the human capacity for physical and psychological survival. As Atwood's painter examines her life through a variety of narratives, a kaleidoscopic personal and sociocultural history develops. *Cat's Eye*, a fictive autobiography of a woman painter, is a novel not simply about Elaine Risley and her shattering personal history as victim and victimiser: it is about the nature of being human in a universe that hardly registers our existence.

PART TWO

SUMMARIES & COMMENTARIES

Cat's Eye *was first published in Toronto by McClelland & Stewart in 1988. It was subsequently published in hardback in the United Kingdom by Bloomsbury Publishing Ltd in 1989, and in paperback by Virago Press in 1990 when it was reprinted four times in the same year.* Cat's Eye *has been regularly reprinted since 1990 by Virago. The edition used in the preparation of this Note is the Virago Press, 1990 edition; the page numbers given throughout the Note will refer equally to all other Virago editions of this novel.*

SYNOPSIS

Cat's Eye is a **fictive autobiography** which tells the story of Elaine Risley, a well-known artist, through a **discursive** account of her life supplied in her 'spoken' narrative, and through a **figural** account of her life developed in her paintings, dreams and visions. Having suffered a period of psychological bullying at the hands of her friends as a child, Elaine has spent most of her life repressing painful memories of a two-year period of victimisation. This brings her close to a state of mental collapse, but her return to Toronto for a retrospective exhibition of her work, forces her to confront her memories, to rationalise them, and finally to forgive her chief persecutor.

The novel is structured around two time-frames. The first involves Elaine's present-tense narrative of her return to contemporary Toronto after a period of twenty years. This narrative traces the events of a few days. The second time-frame involves Elaine's retrospective account of her life, including her Toronto childhood, adolescence, and young adulthood; this narrative covers a period of over thirty years. The novel is divided into fifteen sections, each titled after one of Elaine's paintings (which are described throughout), or after a dominant theme in them. Each section opens with Elaine's present-tense narrative which then flows into her retrospective narrative.

The present-tense narrative deals largely with Elaine's impressions of a renovated, 'World Class' Toronto complete with its fashionable shops and galleries. This narrative also contains several memories of Cordelia since Elaine constantly feels that her childhood friend, who is often characterised in terms of a poltergeist or witch, is lurking unseen. In addition, the present-tense narrative traces Elaine's current relationship with Jon, her ex-husband, whose studio she is occupying for her visit. This narrative culminates in the opening of the retrospective exhibition, and in Elaine's return to the Toronto ravine of her childhood trauma.

The retrospective narrative begins with memories of Elaine's earliest childhood. Elaine traces her family's nomadic years which were happy and carefree. Her brother, Stephen, is her sole childhood companion during this period. Stephen will later develop into a genius and his theoretical **discourses** on astrophysics will prove central to the novel: converted into **metaphors** by Elaine's artist's 'eye', his theories on space-time will provide a subtext to both the discursive and figural narratives.

When the Risley family settle in Toronto at the end of the Second World War, Elaine is introduced into the company of girls for the first time. She attends school and becomes friends with Carol Campbell and with Grace Smeath whose mother is fiercely Protestant. When Cordelia joins the group, Elaine's torment begins. Cordelia and the other girls rigorously 'correct' Elaine who becomes terrified and self-critical as a result. During this period, she feels that her only protection from the girls lies in a cat's eye marble upon which she confers talismanic properties. She also begins to feel that boys are her allies where girls are a deceitful, treacherous enemy.

Elaine's terror finally ends when the girls send her into an icy ravine one day and Elaine almost dies of hypothermia. Believing that she has seen a vision of the Virgin Mary, Elaine finds the will to save her own life and subsequently to break the hold that the girls have over her. Carol, Grace and Cordelia are dismissed from her life, and Elaine achieves a level of stability. However, she only manages this by ruthlessly repressing all her memories of the traumatic two-year period. These years are erased from her conscious mind and transferred to her unconscious, but images from the missing period will later penetrate her dreams and paintings.

Cordelia leaves for a new school but is expelled and returns into Elaine's life when they attend High School together. Power changes hands between them, and Elaine now victimises Cordelia. Elaine does well at school, but Cordelia begins to show clear signs of psychological imbalance. Finally, Cordelia fails her High School exams and suffers a type of nervous breakdown; Elaine refuses to help her, evades her, and finally abandons her.

Elaine attends University where she studies Art and Archaeology and embarks upon an affair with Josef Hrbik, her 'life-drawing' tutor at night-school. Elaine is a regular drinking companion of the male students and begins to sleep with Jon, a fellow-student. Josef, meanwhile, is sleeping with another student, Susie, and when she suffers an agonising abortion, Elaine begins to despise Josef and cruelly rejects him. When she falls accidentally pregnant by Jon, she plunges into mental fragmentation. She recovers, marries Jon, and gives birth to her first daughter. Cordelia contacts Elaine after a period of years; her mental state has disintegrated again and she has been institutionalised following a suicide attempt. Once more, Elaine refuses to help. Cordelia disappears from the novel and is never seen again, but the sense of her presence and a sense of her own guilt haunt Elaine for the rest of the narrative.

Elaine and Jon begin to have increasingly vicious fights, and the marriage finally collapses. Following a half-hearted attempt at suicide as urged by the imagined voice of Cordelia, Elaine and her young daughter leave Toronto, the city of her traumatic youth, to begin a new life in Vancouver. She becomes an established painter, but remains uneasy in the company of women. Elaine has still not recovered her two-year memory-gap and clings on to mental stability despite the continual sense she has that she is about to dissolve into 'nothingness', or fall over an imagined precipice. When she marries her second husband, Ben, she feels that his solidity will ground her. They have a second daughter together. Elaine's paintings continue to provide a figural, autobiographical narrative of her childhood traumas, but she is still unable to decipher the meaning of the images that she paints.

Elaine's brilliant brother is killed by Arab terrorists in a plane hijack, and her parents never recover from the shock. On a visit to her mother before her imminent death, Elaine rediscovers the cat's eye marble of her childhood. As she looks into it, all her repressed memories return in a flash.

The retrospective narrative having been concluded (since we are up-to-date in the story of Elaine's life), the rest of the novel focuses upon the night of the exhibition party, and Elaine's subsequent return to the ravine. Here, she confronts the site of her greatest trauma and buries the 'ghost' of Cordelia in the act of forgiving her. Throughout the novel, an emphasis upon the metaphorical 'twinship' of the two girls has been developed: at this point, Elaine finally manages to sever the connection between them in psychological and emotional terms.

Elaine returns to Vancouver, 'free' of Cordelia and of her memories. However, as she watches two old women giggling on the plane, she understands that she has lost the possibility of a 'future' with Cordelia. Elaine's story is concluded, but the 'way forward' is only dimly seen and remains infused with a sense of loss.

DETAILED SUMMARIES

PREFATORY MATERIAL

The novel is prefaced by two **epigraphs**. The first quotation is taken from Uruguayan writer Eduardo Galeano's *Memory of Fire: Genesis* (Quartet Books, 1985). *Genesis* is the first book in Galeano's trilogy which also includes *Faces and Masks* and *Century of the Wind*. Beginning with Indian creation myths, *Memory of Fire* attempts to trace the psychic roots of contemporary violence in South America.

The epigraph's relevance to *Cat's Eye* lies in the 'twin' **motif** suggested in the quotation. Here, both the murderer and the murdered are annihilated in the act of killing: a merger between the two takes place so that the victim and the victimiser become one. This idea is directly echoed in *Cat's Eye* when Elaine notes that she and Cordelia somehow changed places so that Elaine 'became' Cordelia in a type of psychic exchange of identity and power. The same supernatural exchange that Galeano records in relation to primitive tribes is also involved in European vampire myths (where the victim of the vampire becomes a vampire in turn), and it is no coincidence that the exchange of power between Cordelia and Elaine is effected through such a story (pp. 232–3).

The second epigraph is taken from Stephen Hawking's *A Brief History of Time: From the Big Bang to Black Holes* (Bantam Books, 1988). The question Hawking asks is a rhetorical reference to the fact that the laws of the universe do not correspond to notions of the 'past' and 'future': this is merely how humans respond to the experience of time. Hawking discusses the possibility that time is just as reversible as direction: if we can change direction, why are humans unable to 'remember' the 'future'?

Hawking attempts to answer this question via a complex process of theoretical logic which is of no direct relevance to *Cat's Eye*. Margaret Atwood's narrator understands physics as little as the reader is assumed to do. However, the epigraph is crucial in its suggestion that 'echoes' of the 'future' are contained in the past, as is demonstrated throughout the novel. Elaine's story leads to her realisation that her past, present and future tenses are coexistent, and time is regarded throughout as a series of stacked levels. The Hawking epigraph therefore connects with Elaine's perception and experience of space-time, and with the narrative strategies that develop this crucial theme in *Cat's Eye*.

I: IRON LUNG

Each section in this novel is named after the title of one of Elaine Risley's paintings which are described throughout. *Iron Lung* is one of only two paintings not described in the novel (see also *Bridge*, Section XV). As will later become clear, Elaine is unable to paint this picture because she is still, **metaphorically**, trapped within an 'iron lung', and will continue to be until she can fully confront her memories of childhood trauma. This metaphor will clarify as the novel develops.

CHAPTER 1   Meditations upon the theory of time by the disembodied voice of the narrator

The opening chapter provides a short introduction to one of the central preoccupations of the novel: the theory, and experience, of space-time.

The narrator, Elaine Risley, outlines her brother's explanation of modern theories of space-time; in this theory, time is not a continuum (past-present-future), but is a 'dimension' (see pp. 218–20). It is not linear, so that the past and future coexist with each other. As a result, as the narrator observes, 'Nothing goes away'. Elaine confesses that she has only a partial understanding of this scientific discourse, but it is clear that 'time' will recur throughout the novel as a governing idea (see Themes, on Time).

Readers are given no introduction to the characters at this point, and the subject of the **fictive autobiography** is not made clear. However, central theoretical and metaphorical strands are set into motion in this opening chapter.

'He was already moving away from imprecision of words': Stephen will later reject 'words' in favour of the 'language' of mathematics. Similarly, the narrator will select painting as her career, a medium of communication where the spoken word is redundant.

CHAPTER 2   **The middle-aged Elaine wanders around Toronto, the home of her youth, thinking about her childhood friend, Cordelia**

The meditations upon the theory of time in the previous chapter lead the narrator directly into reminiscence or retrospection. In the present-tense Toronto narrative, the narrator recalls the occasion when she first shared Stephen's theories with her friend, Cordelia. The relationship between the two thirteen-year-olds is superficially close but it is immediately shrouded with ambiguity. In particular, Elaine's description of Cordelia's eyes alerts the reader to the threat ('glinting') and unknowability ('opaque') that Cordelia represents. The narrator tries to picture meeting Cordelia again, and the violence of some of the scenarios she imagines for this encounter indicates that the relationship between them has been traumatic.

Despite Elaine's emphasis on her looks in this chapter and throughout, the reader never manages to develop a clear idea of what Elaine looks like, since her descriptions of herself are vague and mutable, or constantly changing. The theme of metamorphosis will recur throughout the novel, particularly in relation to Elaine and Cordelia.

As Elaine wanders through Toronto, painful memories of her past are triggered. Self-mutilation, in the chewing of her fingers until she draws blood, indicates the extent of the psychological stress that these memories represent.

iron lung a metal casing used to maintain breathing in victims of paralysis. Invented in 1929, the device was used in severe cases of polio
polio poliomyelitis, a potentially fatal viral inflammation attacking the brain and spinal cord

II: SILVER PAPER

The artwork *Silver Paper* is a 'construction' and is described on p. 348. Elaine is a longstanding collector of silver paper, both in her childhood (p. 27) and as an adult (p. 385).

CHAPTER 3   Elaine's assessment of Toronto and a series of 'retrospections'

Elaine is staying at her first husband's apartment in Toronto, her home city, to which she has returned for the retrospective exhibition of her work. Elaine's life and relationships are described in general terms: we learn that she has been married twice, and that she has two 'sensible' daughters. By contrast, Elaine describes herself as disordered, immature and chaotic; Toronto aggravates her self-criticism since, despite its several physical changes, it remains for her a place of 'Malicious, grudging, vindictive, implacable' judgement (p. 14). Elaine's difficult relationship with her identity is indicated in her desire for anonymity, and in her appreciation of her graffitied poster which distorts and disguises her face.

The graffitied moustache on the poster connects with Elaine's desire for metamorphosis since it literally 'defaces' her image and alters it in such a way as to create a new identity.

utilitarianism concerned with usefulness alone without regard to beauty or aesthetic consideration

retrospective an examination of the past; in art, a retrospective exhibition displays the work of an artist to date
Alzheimer's a progressive condition in which nerve cells in the brain degenerate. That this is a disease of the memory (see also p. 263) is significant in terms of the novel as a whole
Kilroy Was Here a generic example of graffiti dating back to the Second World War. See also p. 99

CHAPTER 4   Elaine's memories of her early childhood

Elaine describes her childhood which was spent roaming wartime Canada with her entomologist father, her mother and her older brother. A sense of freedom and happiness is conveyed, and a series of **metaphors** create a strong visual and visceral impression of a nomadic existence lived on the edges of mainstream society.

Several apparently harmless experiences outlined in this chapter will prove significant in terms of the narrator's future trauma. For example, Elaine's war-games with her brother, where 'he can see the enemy and I can't' (p. 25), connect with her later sense of being at the mercy of some lurking threat. Extending the emphasis upon time in this text, the novelist places echoes of the future in memories of the past so that the two coexist as part of the same dimension.

Studebaker an American make of car
LifeSavers a brand of sweet shaped like a ring or life-belt
kapok a light, waterproof, oily fibre used for stuffing pillows and life-belts in particular
Coming in on a wing and a prayer a popular song from the Second World War about Royal Air Force pilots returning home after engaging with the enemy. The 'wing' also connects with the wings of the insects that her father studies. *One Wing* later becomes the title of one of Elaine's paintings (see p. 407)
salamanders tailed amphibian, similar to a lizard
Mercurochrome a deep-red antiseptic

CHAPTER 5   An interlude of childhood memories

Elaine recalls her eighth birthday. A photograph of Elaine provides the reader with a physical description of the tomboy child whose image reminds the adult narrator of immigrants. This anticipates the emphasis upon 'displaced persons' (p. 281) that will be developed throughout the novel.

Elaine remembers reading a schoolbook about a 'typical' American family. Elaine focuses in particular on the image of the girl in the book who is perpetually clean and dressed in conventionally 'feminine' clothes. Elaine begins to long for the company of other girls.

A chapter of intense visual and tactile description.

Several lenses feature in this novel, including a Brownie box-camera, microscopes, telescopes, binoculars and the lens of the eye which will all be centralised at later points. This emphasis upon lenses connects with several themes including painterly vision and scrutiny or judgement (see Themes, on Vision).

Habitant referring to French-Canadian settlers and their way of life

CHAPTER 6   The Risley family moves to Toronto

Elaine's parents buy a house in Toronto where Elaine's father has been made a Professor at the University. Their house is only half-finished, and is hardly a picket-fenced suburban idyll. For the first time in her life, Elaine has a bedroom of her own, but she longs for her 'old rootless life of impermanence and safety' (p. 33).

For Elaine, the only sense of security that she can rely upon is paradoxically connected with the insecurity of transience.

'It fills us with the same kind of rapture' (p. 31) is Elaine's last memory of her life prior to Toronto. The sense of freedom, happiness, and glee communicated here is about to be replaced with misery and inhibition as Elaine is socialised into mainstream society.

CHAPTER 7   Elaine describes her father's laboratories

The chapter begins on the theme of metamorphosis. Elaine's father has been transformed from a scruffy nomad into a besuited Professor; similarly, Elaine's mother, previously dressed in trousers and boots, now wears skirts, stockings and make-up.

Elaine examines her father's students' cross-sectioned diagrams of insects and responds to their visual appeal (this anticipates her future career). On Saturdays, she and Stephen accompany their father to the University laboratories. Elaine describes these rooms in detail, and emphasises the huge scale of the building which is magnified further by the child's viewpoint.

Throughout the 'childhood' sections, the adult narrator is reenacting (or abreacting) scenes from her youth.

Following on from the reference to the camera in Chapter 5, a second type of lens is now introduced: 'two microscopes, old microscopes'.

Witch of Endor see the Bible, 1 Samuel 28:7. A woman with a 'familiar spirit' or devil

planaria flatworms

chitonous skirtlike (Greek, *chiton*)

III: EMPIRE BLOOMERS

In the *Empire Bloomers* series of paintings, Miss Lumley's bloomers become transposed onto images of Mrs Smeath (p. 225, p. 226, p. 404) so that two notions of 'stifling' (p. 226) authority converge. This series of paintings includes 'frightening' (p. 404) images of Mr and Mrs Smeath as copulating insects which are clearly the products of Elaine's chaotic unconscious.

CHAPTER 8   **Back in the present tense, Elaine describes her sense of disembodiment and inner chaos**

The reader is returned to the unhappy voice of the present-tense Elaine who notes that the word '*Nothing*', originally offered as a response to Cordelia's hectoring, is a word she associates with herself. The word 'nothing' connects with the emphasis upon voids and 'black holes' throughout the novel (see Metaphors & Imagery).

It is the day when Elaine's pictures are hung at the gallery. In response to an encroaching depression, Elaine instinctively resorts to attempted disguise and decides to buy herself a new dress for the exhibition's opening night. As she tries on dresses, her bag is almost stolen, and she immediately connects this attempted theft with Cordelia (whose talent for shoplifting will later be outlined). Elaine silently curses her before reminding herself that 'Cordelia is long gone' (p. 44).

Elaine will often refer to her sense of disembodiment throughout the novel: 'handling my arms and legs as if they're someone else's' (p. 42). Her 'disembodied' voice on the answaphone has been emphasised on p. 41.

'What I'd like to be is transformed ... Disguise is easier ...' (p. 44): the emphasis upon metamorphosis and disguise recurs. This theme will also be carried into the idea of 'performance' in later chapters.

CHAPTER 9   Elaine returns to her retrospective narrative: at school, gendered rules are beginning to be learned

The childhood narrative continues with Elaine's memories of her first days at Queen Mary Public School. This is a segregated environment where boys and girls enter the building via different doorways before filing into the same classrooms: an illogical custom that 'baffles' the young Elaine. Through her new female friend, Carol Campbell, Elaine learns of the world of hairdressers and of romance, and learns that she does not own the 'correct' clothes. In Carol's descriptions at school of Elaine's home-life, Elaine is likened to an alien species, unfamiliar with the customs of mainstream society.

The learning of gendered behaviour dominates this chapter.

Never having been in the company of girls – '... with girls I sense ... unforeseen, calamitous blunder' (p. 47) – Elaine feels like an outsider, and her sense that she is always on the verge of some terrible error will later be capitalised upon by Cordelia. The adult Elaine continues to feel vulnerable in the presence of women.

ravine a deep, narrow gorge that will later become centralised (see Textual Analysis)

CHAPTER 10   Elaine's lessons in gendered behaviour become
increasingly subtle

Elaine introduces Carol to her father's laboratories. Carol reacts
squeamishly and, although Elaine feels that Carol is behaving like a
'sissy', she also feels approval and pride at her friend's 'delicacy'.
Elaine is given a series of guided tours around Carol's house. Carol
introduces Elaine to her friend Grace Smeath. Being a year older than
the other girls, Grace is firmly in control of the games they play. These
games all involve indoor activities such as creating collages of women
surrounded by domestic appliances cut from a mail order catalogue.
Elaine learns the subtleties of female behaviour including the feigning of
modesty.

An emphasis on twins and doubleness occurs in this section, with
twin-set, twin beds, and the words 'twin-like', 'identical', and
'doubleness' following each other in swift succession.

Pretending that all female efforts are substandard is defined by
the novelist here as a basic 'code' of female behaviour: '... and say
I've done it badly. Partly this is a relief' (p. 54). While Elaine
acknowledges that this opting out from more obviously competitive
'male' pursuits, is a 'relief', the word 'partly' potentially suggests
ambivalence.

cold wave a type of perm

CHAPTER 11   An introduction to Mrs Smeath and to her 'bad heart'

It is now Christmas, and Elaine is given a red handbag as a present.
Elaine's addiction to comics is described; she becomes particularly
fascinated with cartoon characters who have 'round holes for eyes',
who have 'secret identities', and who are able to metamorphose at
will.
Elaine is growing closer to Grace Smeath and becomes familiar
with her mother who suffers from a 'bad heart'. At the end of the chapter,
the adult Elaine seems confused by the 'hate' she still feels for Mrs
Smeath: only when she confronts her childhood memories in full will she
be able to account for this bitterness.

Though Mrs Smeath's bad heart indicates physical ill-health at this stage, the phrase will later be extended to suggest a vindictive, judgemental nature.

Connecting with the emphasis upon the 'twinship' of Elaine and Cordelia, a **metaphor** for their relationship will develop in the suggestion that the two girls are as a negative is to a print: two versions of the same image, neither is complete without the other: 'everything that's white in the real picture is black in the negative' (p. 55). (See Themes, on Gothic.)

A child's inability to understand abstract ideas is captured in 'like rot in an apple or a bruise' (p. 58). Elaine resorts to a visual metaphor as she is unable to grasp the nature of invisible disease.

Oxfords sturdy, practical, lace-up shoes
antimacassar covering for chairbacks

CHAPTER 12   Changing seasons, children's games, and the 'cat's eye' marbles

The narrator outlines the range of children's games she remembers playing. When marbles are introduced into the schoolyard (the only game that both the girls and the boys play in this novel), Elaine becomes obsessed with a blue 'cat's eye' marble which she keeps in her red bag. Stephen is an accomplished player of marbles, wins a huge collection, and mysteriously buries his 'treasure' along with a map that pinpoints its location.

'They're the eyes of something that isn't known but exists anyway' (p. 62): the 'cat's eye' of the title is a multi-faceted **symbol** (see Themes, on Vision; and Metaphors & Imagery). The idea of something existing that is unknown and unnamed is deliberately unsettling.

Salome see the Bible, Matthew 14. Salome was the daughter of Herodius who, following an erotic dance, demanded the head of John the Baptist by way of reward

y

CHAPTER 13   A summer interlude in the wilderness while the
storm approaches in the shape of Cordelia

When the summer arrives, the Risleys return to the wilderness as
Elaine's father is observing a caterpillar infestation in Northern
Canada. Elaine is reluctantly torn from her 'new life, the life of girls',
but finds that, before long, she can hardly even picture Grace and
Carol. She is briefly unsettled when she observes her parents within
their camping hut and becomes aware that 'It's as if I don't exist' (p. 68).
Even at this stage, Elaine is beginning to experience a sense of ghostly
disembodiment.

When the family returns home at the end of the summer, a third
girl has joined Grace and Carol. Though Elaine is 'empty of premonition'
when she sees the new girl, the fact that the word 'premonition' is
mentioned implies that something sinister is sure to be connected with
the unknown newcomer.

In the final paragraph of this chapter, words associated with eyes
and sight recur in connection with Cordelia ('stare', 'look', 'seen'). A sense
of threat is conveyed.

'Our father has shed his city clothing ...' (p. 65): shape-shifting,
or metamorphosis, is again implied. Caterpillars being the
insects most associated with metamorphosis, Professor Risley's
entomological specialism becomes significant.

The novelist incorporates Elaine's father's voice into that of the
child, 'if he were a betting man, he says, he'd put his money on the
insects' (p. 66), thus creating the impression of a child's mimicry of
adult phrases which are only half-understood.

CHAPTER 14   The reader is introduced to Cordelia and to her
strange world: relationships develop

Elaine describes her first impressions of Cordelia. Despite her initial
uncertainty upon meeting the stranger, Elaine finds herself being drawn
into a 'circle of two' with her.

Elaine describes Cordelia's luxurious household which is dominated
by Cordelia's vaguely menacing father. The youngest of three sisters,
Cordelia is painfully aware that she is a 'disappointment' to her 'gifted'

family. Cordelia is particularly drawn towards play-acting and the ghoulish; she tells the girls that the stream in the ravine consists of 'dissolved dead people'. Together with the discarded condom that the girls find one day, the ravine becomes connected with a sense of supernatural menace and of threat.

Cordelia's father (the reader never learns the family's surname) is a subtly threatening presence, 'He is large, craggy, charming, but we have heard him shouting, upstairs' (p. 73). With the exception of Professor Risley, most fathers in these childhood sections of the novel are connected with punishment and discipline.

The moustache Cordelia draws on herself echoes the graffitied moustache on Elaine's poster in Chapter 3.

The lethal properties of 'deadly nightshade, its berries red as valentine candies' (p. 74) are made more sinister still by the harmless way in which the vivid crimson berries are described. Cordelia will also later insist that a single drop of juice from these berries can 'turn you into a zombie'.

Giselle a classical ballet by Adolphe Adam (1803–56)

safe condom

CHAPTER 15   The terrors of Miss Lumley and her horrifying 'bloomers'

One of Elaine's teachers, the terrifying Miss Lumley, is remembered by the adult Elaine. Miss Lumley is a sadistic disciplinarian who is rumoured to wear 'dark, mysterious, repulsive bloomers'. To Elaine as a child, the fear inspired by this woman becomes inextricably associated with these hideous bloomers which seem to contaminate the atmosphere in some insidious way. This in turn becomes connected with Miss Lumley's extreme Imperialist rhetoric complete with mythologised images of the British Royal Family.

The bloomers represent to Elaine fear, disgust, and half-understood ideological indoctrination, as the title of this section suggests ('bloomers' can also imply 'blunders' or 'errors'). What further disturbs Elaine is her realisation that she is implicated in the disturbing secrets suggested by Miss Lumley's bloomers since she and her teacher are both female.

Referring to Miss Lumley's bloomers, 'whatever is wrong with them may be wrong with me also' (p. 81), Elaine is generalising their horror to encompass a perceived 'wrongness' with the state of being female.

Rule Britannia popular, patriotic song by Thomas Arne, originally from the musical drama *Alfred* (1740)
Wolfe General James Wolfe (*d.* 1759), who died taking Quebec from the French

IV: DEADLY NIGHTSHADE

The painting *Deadly Nightshade* is described on p. 337. Images connected with Deadly Nightshade recur throughout the novel. The lethal plant can be read as a **metaphor** for the 'poison' that contaminates Elaine's childhood.

CHAPTER 16   **At 'Sub-Versions', Elaine inspects her paintings, and baits a journalist**

In the present-tense narrative, Elaine visits the 'Sub-Versions' gallery and views a painting of Mrs Smeath (*Rubber Plant: The Ascension*) which depicts the subject in a **parodic** ascension fantasy . Discussing the placing of her pictures on the gallery walls, Elaine indicates that she favours a chronological progression (continuing the theme of time). In the presence of the glamorous exhibition organisers, Elaine feels middle-aged and oddly under attack. These feelings increase when she is 'ambushed' into talking to a journalist about her work. As a result, she reacts aggressively to the journalist's questions about her **feminist** commitment (which she denies having), and about her motivation. She becomes increasingly uncomfortable and begins to pick at her fingers in a return of an old habit of self-mutilation.

Elaine characteristically views herself as an 'alien' or a 'displaced person', 'as if they are a species of which I am not a member' (see

p. 87 and also p. 281). This partly results from her late socialisation as a child.

'I hate party lines, I hate ghettos' (p. 90): Elaine's aggression is a result of her feelings of vulnerability, but her resistance to the feminist label is genuine. On pp. 378–9, Elaine's position is clarified further; at both points, Elaine's ambivalence about feminism becomes connected with her hostile feelings towards women in general.

The entire narrative leads towards a confrontation with this one question 'Why do you paint?' (p. 91). It is only when Elaine can understand the nature of her memories that are coded within the pictures that she is able to confront the issue of why she is compelled to paint.

'cut off my ear' referring to the Dutch painter Vincent Van Gogh (1853–90)

egg tempera a paint made of egg yolk and pigment (see Chapter 58)

The Ascension in Christian mythology, Jesus 'ascended' into Heaven after his death

iconoclasm the act of destroying images that are the object of religious or ideological worship or veneration

succubus a devil that assumes a female body to have sex with men in their sleep

CHAPTER 17   Cordelia introduces Elaine, Grace and Carol to the 'facts' of life

Cordelia has no patience for the game of cutting out consumer durables from the Eaton's catalogue: she is, however, interested in the underwear section of the catalogue since she is fascinated with breasts. She defaces the underwear models with moustaches (see also p. 20 and p. 74) while she outlines to the girls her inaccurate 'facts' about menstruation and sex. Elaine is appalled by most of what she hears. As on p. 81, she is disturbed by the idea that she is connected through her gender with the physical characteristics of adult womanhood which she describes as 'alien' and 'monstrous'.

Elaine's mind has been focused upon the mating habits of various insects, and these thoughts become transposed onto the idea of Mr and Mrs Smeath having sex: 'I think of Mr and Mrs Smeath, stark naked, with Mr Smeath stuck to the back of Mrs Smeath' (p. 95). This explains the connections the adult Elaine represents in the painting *Erbug, The Annunciation*, described on p. 225.

the curse slang for the menstrual period
ovipositors egg-laying organs in female insects and some female fishes

CHAPTER 18   **The Smeath family introduce Elaine to religion**

Sensing a heathen, Mrs Smeath invites Elaine to their church on Sunday with the Smeath family. Elaine finds this new 'dimension' fascinating. In **ironic** counterpoint to biblical inscriptions on paintings (*Suffer the Little Children*) is the graffiti that adorns the entrance to the Sunday School (see also p. 20).

To indulge Mr Smeath, a visit to the train track follows church. Elaine then attends the Smeath Sunday lunch where Mr Smeath is revealed to be less rigid and more jovial than his forbidding wife.

That night, Elaine contemplates the nature of Heaven.

A sinister shadow intrudes in the final lines of the chapter when the previously benign-looking stars become **symbols** of judgement and watchfulness.

The image of an onion, 'there's a thing that looks like an onion' (p. 98), recurs in the painting, *Erbug, the Annunciation* (p. 225).

white bird in Christian symbolism, representing the Holy Spirit
KINGDOM-OF-GOD Bible, Luke 17:21
SUFFER-THE-LITTLE-CHILDREN Bible, Mark 10:14. The word 'suffer' in this context means 'allow' ('allow the little children to come unto me'), but the more usual meaning of the word has clear application in terms of Elaine's later experiences
THE-GREATEST-OF-THESE Bible, Corinthians 13:13. St Paul speaking of the three theological virtues, Faith, Hope and Charity
Doxology a hymn or liturgical formula ascribing glory to God

CHAPTER 19   Stephen develops an interest in astronomy

In the schoolyard, the rules of gender difference continue to be learned: the boys, for example, 'work at acting like boys' (pp. 102–3). Meanwhile, Stephen experiences his first crush on a girl, and Elaine is mystified as to why this attachment should turn him into a 'more nervous identical twin of himself' (p. 103). Stephen subsequently diverts his energies towards astronomy, and his mania for collections is manifested in his 'collecting' of stars. Elaine is aware that the stars of his scientific universe are perceived in radically different terms to the 'watchful' stars of the religious universe.

Elaine's autobiographical paintings can be regarded as a form of 'invisible writing': 'There's invisible writing that comes out ...' (p. 104). The images represent a type of **allegorical**, 'invisible' language that needs to be deciphered by the reader and by Elaine herself.

The range of lenses indicated earlier is extended here to include binoculars and telescopes. Together with the earlier camera and microscope, and bearing in mind the emphasis upon the lens of the eye, each represents degrees of magnification.

bangs American term: in English, 'fringe'
light-years see also speed of light, Chapter 68. This continues the meditations upon the nature of time as introduced in Chapter 1
Arcturus one of the brightest stars in the Northern Hemisphere

CHAPTER 20   Hallowe'en, and a crucial gap in memory

The girls go trick-or-treating on Hallowe'en. Subsequently, Elaine is dressed as Mary Queen of Scots in a game: having supposedly been beheaded, she is buried by the girls in a deep hole that Cordelia has been digging in her back garden. When Elaine realises that the girls have run away and left her in the mock-grave, she panics: she has, in effect, been 'buried alive' (see Themes, on Gothic). Looking back on the event, Elaine can remember 'nothing' about being in the hole (the **irony** of the preceding emphasis upon 'Remembrance' Day is implicit), though she can locate it as 'The point at which I lost power' (p. 107). At the end of the chapter, she struggles to 'picture' the 'right' memories of being trapped in the hole, but a blank that indicates profound trauma persists.

'*The witches are out*' (p. 106) is one of a chain of references in this novel to witches and to witchcraft; on p. 90, for example, Elaine mentions the 'witch-and-succubus' pieces that have been written about her, 'Voodoo and spells' occur on p. 112, and the spells of Shakespeare's *Macbeth* are echoed on p. 113. Cordelia and Elaine are the characters most associated with this emphasis.

Elaine's description of non-memory, '… only a black square filled with nothing' (p. 107), also describes the 'black square' of time that her conscious mind has repressed.

V: WRINGER

The painting titled *Wringer* is described on p. 337. Elaine connects this instrument with torture and pain (see p. 123 and p. 180).

CHAPTER 21   Elaine goes shopping in Toronto: memories of self-maiming

Upon leaving the art gallery after the fraught interview, Elaine decides to go shopping. In a department store, she reveals herself to be an obsessive buyer of make-up and creams. Inspecting children's party dresses made of tartan fabric, Elaine recalls quotations from Shakespeare's *Macbeth*; the thought of Lady Macbeth then triggers images of 'slippery' little girls in Elaine's mind.

Elaine tells how, in the midst of the terrors Cordelia caused, she would deliberately maim and mutilate herself. Elaine rejoices that her own daughters are almost alarmingly sane. She indicates that she was once afraid that she would unwittingly damage her daughters through her very presence in their lives.

Elaine describes the world of the cosmetics counters in two principal ways: first, she uses military terms such as 'war' and 'regimes'; this in turn becomes connected with religion and intersects with witchcraft: 'This is religion. Voodoo and spells', and 'slug juice, toad spit, eye of newt' (this recalling the witches' brew of

Macbeth, IV.1.15: 'Eye of newt and toe of frog'). Elaine's passionate devotion to cosmetics connects with her ceaseless search for disguise and metamorphosis.

As a child, Elaine's body had become a type of 'canvas' upon which her inner pain could be physically etched and expressed: 'why bite something that didn't hurt?' (p. 114). In one sense, she had 'written' her inner conflict upon her body so that the stigmatic wounds on her feet and hands became an embodiment of her invisible pain.

metastasizes moves from one organ to another
My way of life ... Macbeth, V.3 (see Literary Background)
plaid American for 'tartan'

CHAPTER 22   **Psychological warfare begins**

Elaine, newly disempowered in the group of girls, has become the victim of a sustained course of 'self-improvement', designed and implemented by her 'friends'. Signs that this is leading to psychological disturbance are legion, but Elaine conceals her misery from her parents. Accomplished dissemblers and hypocrites, the girls are models of well-mannered innocence when in the presence of adults. In later life, Elaine anxiously scrutinises her own daughters for signs of either victimhood or of a similar 'hypocrisy'.

Both as a child and as an adult, Elaine is unable to express her trauma **discursively**, or in words: 'Even to myself I am mute' (p. 117). Her need for a **figural** mode of communication via painting clearly connects with her discursive 'muteness'.

As Elaine distances herself from the menace of what she is about to confront, the theme of disembodiment is sustained: 'I look at the closed door, at the doorknob, at my own hand moving up, as if it's no longer a part of me' (p. 118). Several of Elaine's paintings depicting figures who are defying gravity and who appear to float free of their bodies, develop this theme further.

CHAPTER 23   **Elaine's embarrassed complicity with Mr Smeath**

To avoid her friends, Elaine volunteers for domestic chores and becomes particularly fascinated with wringing the laundry. She imagines her arm being passed through the machine, followed by her whole body, emerging flat the other side.

At a Smeath family Sunday lunch, Mr Smeath makes a vulgar joke about beans; he senses an ally in Elaine and tries to implicate her in the joke. She feels 'trapped' in a no-win situation, but Elaine's alignment with men, who do not judge her, is increasing in direct proportion to her suspicion of women.

Throughout the novel, Elaine constantly feels that she is about to stumble over an imagined edge or precipice, or cross an unseen line: 'At any time I may step over some line I don't even know is there' (p. 121) is an example.

CHAPTER 24   Christmas dinner with another 'displaced person'

Cordelia takes her first acting part when she plays a weasel in a production of *The Wind in the Willows*. Elaine is terrified by not being able to tell where Cordelia is on stage. Cordelia's capacity to be simultaneously absent and present is indicated here and suggests a spectral or poltergeist identity (see Themes, on Gothic, and Characters).

The Risleys entertain a guest at Christmas dinner; Mr Banerji is a student of Professor Risley, visiting from India. As such, he is a 'displaced person' (see p. 281), and Elaine feels an instinctive affinity with him. Whilst eating the wing of the domesticated turkey that has had its ability to fly reared out of it, Elaine realises that she is 'eating lost flight'.

Further images of 'lost flight' will recur throughout the novel.

sternum breast-bone. It is here also that Elaine feels 'Something tight' (p. 119) that prevents her from eating

Meleagris gallopavo Latin name for the turkey

CHAPTER 25   Elaine encounters antiSemitism for the first time

Elaine is employed by a neighbour, the exotic Mrs Finestein, to take her baby out in his baby-carriage each day. Cordelia and the girls reveal that the Finesteins are Jewish, and Grace and Carol mimic the antisemitic sentiments of their parents. Elaine understands that she must sacrifice her job if the baby's safety is to be guaranteed since she cannot trust the girls not to put him in danger.

In a particularly offensive trap, Cordelia leads Elaine into calling her father a 'bugger': Elaine does not fully understand what she has said, but she is aware that 'I have betrayed, I have been betrayed' (p. 135). The word is later transposed onto the picture *Erbug, The Annunciation* (p. 225) in the coded form of '*Erbug*' (a near anagram of 'bugger').

It is significant that one of the few women in this novel for whom Elaine feels unambiguous warmth is a 'displaced person' (p. 281). Miss Stuart (who will be introduced later) is another 'displaced person' with whom Elaine connects, and she and Mrs Finestein appear together in the painting *Three Muses* (pp. 406–7).

kikes racist term for Jews

CHAPTER 26   **Elaine discovers sickness to be a temporary sanctuary**

Falling ill with gastroenteritis, Elaine accidentally stumbles upon a way of avoiding the girls, and she begins to fake illness regularly. Propped up in bed, she cuts out images of women from magazines, concentrating on the ones who are tackling some physical imperfection (spots, greasy hair and so on). Cartoons depicting a 'Watchbird', designed to warn women against 'female' faults such as nagging, fill Elaine with anxiety because they represent yet another form of all-seeing judgement.

During her numerous convalescences, Elaine listens to the 'Happy Gang' on the radio, but she finds that she does not trust their apparent 'happiness'. She also listens to the Official Time Signal, but begins to dread the lull before one o'clock strikes: the pause suggests that 'time is passing', and that the future is imminent. Elaine fears this future and so turns her head into the pillow so as to avoid hearing its arrival.

'This is a Watchbird watching YOU' (p. 138) was a regular feature of women's magazines of the 1940s and 1950s, the 'Watchbird' is a relic from the novelist's own childhood. Such details contribute to the strong sense of social documentary in this novel.

CHAPTER 27   **The cat's eye marble becomes Elaine's talisman**

Elaine retreats into a realm of private **symbols**: the cat's eye marble becomes a type of talisman or protector (see Metaphors & Imagery), and Elaine increasingly feels that she is seeing through the 'pure' lens of the cat's eye marble. As such, she feels that 'I am alive in my eyes only' (p. 141).

Summer in the wilderness begins to 'heal' Elaine, physically and psychologically. However, when she finds a dead raven (another symbol of 'lost flight', p. 131), she realises that death connotes an inviolable space beyond pain, and she becomes attracted to states of void or non-being. A series of highly disturbing dreams recurring throughout the Summer are detailed. Elaine notes that none of these dreams are about Cordelia, but, in fact, *all* of them are 'about her' in some way.

VI: CAT'S EYE

The painting of this name is a self-portrait involving mirrors. The background detail of the painting shows three small girls dressed in 1940s clothes walking through snow (recalling the events of p. 137). Although there are no cat's eyes in the painting as described, its title may refer to the way in which the subject's eyes are painted.

CHAPTER 28   **Elaine rescues an old woman from the pavement**

In the present-tense narrative, Elaine is appalled by the sugary excess of the food on offer in the 'world class' food hall. This leads her to recall the postwar austerity of her youth, and this in turn triggers thoughts of her mother. Elaine considers the painting *Pressure Cooker* which she had completed following her mother's death. *Pressure Cooker* is a 'double triptych' series of paintings depicting Mrs Risley occupied in various tasks. Elaine resists a **feminist** interpretation of the series, and indicates that it was simply an attempt to make her mother 'timeless'.

In the street, Elaine assists an old woman who has fallen to the pavement. The woman is drunk and, in an alcoholic 'vision', mistakes Elaine for the Virgin Mary. Elaine offers her money, tries to interpret this gesture as a sign of her 'goodness', but instantly feels that she is less 'good' than 'vengeful, greedy, secretive and sly'.

'I'm a bleeding heart' (p. 153) will later be echoed in a chain of **metaphors** circulating around images of the heart and of the Virgin Mary who is traditionally depicted in Catholic iconography with a blood-stained wound in her chest. The phrase is an idiomatic expression, meaning someone whose compassion is easily tapped.

bas-relief a type of sculpture with figures standing out slightly from the background
triptych a set of pictures on three panels, usually hinged side by side; triptychs are particularly associated with religious paintings

CHAPTER 29   Elaine refuses to confide in her mother when the opportunity arises

As soon as the Risleys return home to Toronto, Elaine can feel her body 'emptying itself of feeling' as she becomes trapped in a terrifying 'future' (shifting tenses are often indicated via the symbol of doors in this novel, as here). Cordelia's campaign of victimisation continues, and Elaine feels as though she is being backed towards the edge of a cliff. In Grade 5 at school, Elaine and Carol have a new teacher; Miss Stuart is a significant improvement upon Miss Lumley.

Elaine's mother has finally noticed the signs of her daughter's distress, but confesses that she has no idea how to help her. Instead, she advises Elaine to develop 'backbone', or strength of character. When her mother provides an opening for Elaine to confide in her, Elaine refuses to tell on the grounds that, if she does, 'what little backbone I have left will crumble away to nothing' (p. 157).

'I am too numb, too enthralled,' Elaine thinks on p. 155. This 'numbness' is an attempt at emotional detachment. The word 'enthralled' continues the chain of references to witchcraft and sorcery throughout the novel since Elaine is evidently in 'thrall' to Cordelia and has been trapped by a type of 'spell'.

CHAPTER 30   Princess Elizabeth visits Toronto

Cordelia brings a mirror to school, and uses it to further erode Elaine's self-confidence. Elaine describes her parents' 'bridge parties' which confuse her since 'bridges' seem not to be involved (Elaine's childish, literal mind is again in evidence here). Mr Banerji is a guest at these parties and Elaine waits for his arrival so that she can check that this other 'displaced person' is surviving.

Princess Elizabeth is on a State Visit to Canada and it is announced that she will visit Toronto. Elaine places great faith in this visit as if the mythic bravery of this girl will somehow effect a profound change in her own life. However, the car bearing the Princess passes by quickly and Elaine finds no magical transformation in her situation has occurred.

The faith that Elaine places in the icon of Princess Elizabeth anticipates the faith that she will place in her ultimate female 'rescuer', the Virgin Mary (see Chapter 35).

CHAPTER 31   **For the first time, Elaine paints a picture that she does not understand**

Miss Stuart instructs her pupils to draw a picture of what they do after school, and Elaine inadvertently produces an almost blacked-out image of herself in bed. She cannot account for how or why she has produced this picture.

Elaine is inundated with Valentine's Day messages, and interprets the messages as evidence that boys are her 'secret allies'. Elaine's mother miscarries a baby and Elaine dreams of the dead child which she regards as having been one of a pair of twins. Elaine also dreams that the two 'displaced persons', Mrs Finestein and Mr Banerji, are her real parents. In the most disturbing dream of the sequence, Elaine dreams that her mother and father are simultaneously dead and alive, and are sinking into the earth watching her as they recede.

When Miss Stuart looks at Elaine's picture and says 'I see', she is indicating that she has deciphered the accidental image in precise terms: she not only 'sees' the picture in visual terms, but she has also understood it (in the dual meaning of 'I see'). Elaine will herself echo these words, and the double-meaning implicit in them, on p. 404.

a rubber thing a diaphragm, as used in birth control

CHAPTER 32   **Elaine finds a way of escaping 'time'**

Elaine's father's university department is holding a Conversat, a scientific exhibition open to the public. The exhibits all connect with ideas circulating in Elaine's mind either prior to, or following, this day:

on display, for example, is a jar containing a pair of dead twins, and this echoes Elaine's dream about her mother's miscarriage in Chapter 31. The heat of the building causes Elaine to faint; she discovers this to be a much-needed escape route since it involves moving 'out of time or into another time' (p. 171).

Elaine's torments at the hands of Cordelia and the girls continue. Forced to stand alone by a wall one day, Elaine experiments with her fainting technique and undergoes an 'out of body' experience. Elaine subsequently perfects the art of 'spending time' outside her body without even having to black out.

In the phrase 'I feel blurred, as if there are two of me ...' (p. 173) the word 'blurred' suggests the image of a smudgy photographic print, while the sense of duality connects with the emphasis upon twinship throughout.

pig Latin this is another 'secret language' in this novel of codes and ciphers. In 'pig Latin', words are formed by reversing syllables and adding the suffix 'ay'

VII: OUR LADY OF PERPETUAL HELP

The title of this section refers to a Catholic name for the Virgin Mary who is depicted in a painting described on p. 345. Elaine will later develop a profound connection with the idea of the Virgin Mary; she believes that she has experienced a 'vision' of her in the ravine, and ideas and symbols of her seem to pursue Elaine into adult life (see p. 153 for one example that has been provided prior to this).

CHAPTER 33   Memories of life with Jon

In the present tense (as at the beginning of each section), Elaine scans a telephone directory for the names of her childhood friends and former lover, but finds no trace of anyone except the Campbells.

Elaine recalls the early phases of her relationship with Jon. She relates an incident where a girlfriend of his had walked in on them while in bed together, and had hurled a bag of hot spaghetti at them. Jon is clearly a serial two-timer, but Elaine had not realised this at the time. She secretly admires the 'courage' of the outraged intruder and notes that it would be many years before she would be able to claim a similar 'courage' herself.

The series of imagined or perceived transgressions onto 'forbidden' territory that echoes throughout the novel is implied in 'there was a line you crossed' (p. 178).

CHAPTER 34   Elaine learns the meaning of 'hate'

After Sunday lunch at the Smeaths, Elaine overhears Mrs Smeath and Aunt Mildred discussing her. They reveal that they are aware of the psychological abuse to which Elaine is being subjected by the girls. Not only do they condone this abuse, but they also 'relish' the idea of it. Hate enters Elaine 'like a kick', and she imagines Mrs Smeath being passed through the wringer by way of revenge.

Elaine has 'lost confidence' in God who has failed to come to her rescue. When she finds a religious image of the Virgin Mary on the pavement, the title, *The Lady of Perpetual Help*, encourages Elaine and she decides to pray to her in future. Kneeling by her bed, Elaine squeezes her eyes together in the attempt to summon up a vision of the Virgin and manages to produce an image of the external heart which recalls her red plastic purse.

The connection between the heart, 'eyes', and judgement becomes explicit in 'Her bad heart floats in her body like an eye, an evil eye, it sees me' (p. 180). In addition, Mrs Smeath's 'bad heart' will be counterpointed by the externalised, pierced heart of the Virgin Mary in the religious image that Elaine finds.

burdock a weed that grows in the ravine

God sees the little sparrow fall ... see the Bible, Matthew 10:29–31, and Luke 12:7. This idea recalls the sense of the all-seeing eyes of God

The Seven Sorrows in the Catholic faith, these refer to the 'sorrows' that 'transfixed' the heart of Mary; in Catholic iconography, the **metaphorical** image is usually represented literally in the depiction of an external and bleeding heart (hence the term, 'bleeding heart', as used on p. 153)

CHAPTER 35   Elaine's 'vision' in the ravine

The girls play after school in the March snow. When Cordelia accidentally falls, her mood darkens, and Elaine becomes the butt of her fury. Cordelia throws her snow hat into the ravine and orders Elaine to retrieve it. Having slipped down the treacherous hill, Elaine falls into the icy water that is said to flow straight from the cemetery. Cordelia and the girls have long since run away. Clearly hypothermic and panic-stricken by her experiences, Elaine lapses into semiconsciousness before apparently seeing a vision of the Virgin Mary. The vision wordlessly communicates the words '*It will be all right. Go home*'.

> When Cordelia leaves her impression in the snow, it can be said that this represents a **metaphor** for her entire character. So insubstantial is she that an imprint becomes her 'signature'. As such, Cordelia is consistently defined in terms of partial presence, or semi-absence. (See also Textual Analysis, Text 1.)

CHAPTER 36   Elaine frees herself from the girls

Elaine manages to struggle home and subsequently suffers from a brief fever. Back at school, she is accused of having 'told' on the girls (she has not done so), but she suddenly discovers the courage to turn her back on her persecutors. She has realised that Cordelia's games have all been based upon 'imitation', 'acting' and 'impersonation'. As she leaves the girls, she understands that they need her far more than she needs them as, without her, they are robbed of their victim, the figure onto whom their own anxieties can be projected. Cordelia, Grace and Carol find themselves relegated to the margins of Elaine's life despite their attempts to lure back their victim.

> Elaine and Cordelia are represented as two animals in the image 'Cordelia circles me warily. I catch her eyes on me, considering ...' (p. 192). In addition, Cordelia's manipulative mind is indicated in her calculating eyes.

> Previously, Elaine has consciously constructed an external protective layer, in resorting to cat's eye vision and, through it, emotional detachment. Now, however, the protective layer is

internal: 'There's something hard in me, crystalline, a kernel of glass' (p. 193).

VIII: half a face

This title refers to one of Elaine's paintings of Cordelia. The picture echoes the disturbing story of the twins related on p. 211, and also involves Elaine's dream of Cordelia who appears holding her head in a cloth (p. 360).

CHAPTER 37   **Elaine finds the 'Virgin of lost things', but is unsure of what she has 'lost'**

Elaine explains that she spent many years visiting churches looking for images of the Virgin Mary, unconsciously searching for a representation of the Virgin that matched her vision in the ravine. In an unusually subdued Mexican church, she had found such an image: the 'Virgin of lost things' depicted here is dressed in black, as was the figure in Elaine's vision.

Elaine recalls that her daughters had passed through an irritating adolescent phase of responding to adult questions with a bored and insolent '*So?*' Cordelia had adopted the same response at a similar age. Elaine imagines saying to Cordelia, 'You made me believe I was nothing', and being met with a stubborn, 'blank-eyed', '*So?*' (p. 199).

Elaine's visit to Mexico with Ben occurs 'between' the two 'framing' narratives of 'childhood' and 'present day'.

In the phrase, 'You made me believe I was nothing' (p. 199 and see also p. 41), 'nothing' links with Elaine's childhood sense of self-protective 'numbness', and also refers to paralysing feelings of self-hate that have dogged Elaine ever since.

To which there is no answer not only is '*So?*' answerless (because there is no question as such), but also 'there is no answer' because Cordelia is absent

CHAPTER 38   Elaine develops amnesia; high school and a
              reintroduction to Cordelia

Time speeds up in this chapter and a full year is traced within it. The
sense of a new phase of personal and cultural history is created with the
death of George VI and the accession of Queen Elizabeth.

Elaine cannot recall the details of her traumatic years since she has
repressed the painful memories. While this repression is a survival
mechanism, its negative longterm implications are indicated in the phrase
'*Happy as a clam*' (p. 201); as Elaine points out, 'happy' here is connected
with 'hard-shelled, firmly closed', and it therefore carries negative
implications.

In preparation for High School, Elaine clears out her bedroom and
stores the remnants of her childhood in the cellar. Cordelia returns to the
neighbourhood and to Elaine's school, having been expelled from her
private school. A year older than Elaine, she looks like a sophisticated
teenager which makes Elaine feel that 'I look like a kid dressed up as one'
(p. 204).

> Notice 'a solitary cat's eye marble' (p. 203). Had Elaine referred to
> 'the' marble, she would be marking it out as 'special' and unique. By
> referring to 'a' marble, however, she is indicating that the item is of
> no particular significance. The extent of her repressed memory is
> communicated in this one word.

> 'She has vanished completely' (p. 204): Cordelia 'vanishes' so
> frequently in this novel, and is absent for so much of it, that her
> presence is only ever partial at best.

CHAPTER 39   Elaine and Cordelia during their High School years

Elaine and Cordelia attend Burnham High School; this name continues
a chain of references to Shakespeare's *Macbeth* in this novel (Birnam
Wood is the site indicated in the Witches' prophecy in that play). Despite
feeling that she is 'acting' a role, Elaine joins Cordelia in standard teenage
pursuits. Cordelia, meanwhile, is still subject to relentless disapproval
from her family. She begins shoplifting, and she and Elaine become
addicted to horror comics. The most significant story they encounter in
terms of the novel as a whole involves a tale of two twins, one pretty, one

scarred. Other stories involve a host of ghosts and zombies, stranded
between life and death (see Themes, on Gothic).

Elaine's disgusted reaction to signs of femaleness indicates an
almost pathological level of anxiety about her own gender in
her: 'the skin of their faces is slippery-looking, slick with oily juice'
(p. 207 and see also p. 81).

The story of the twins echoes through the novel and appears in
allegorical terms in the painting *Half a Face*. In its emphasis upon
twinship and doubles, it connects in particular with the **Gothic**
elements of this narrative.

CHAPTER 40   **Elaine's home and family; an introduction to**
              theoretical physics

This chapter supplies information on three important levels: it
provides an update on the Risley family's home life and on the
developing relationships within the family unit; it traces the process of
Elaine's psychology during this period; and it reintroduces and
expands the connections between Stephen's discourse upon theoretical
physics and the **metaphorical** design of both **discursive** and **figural**
narratives.

The sense of Cordelia's defining presence/absence as shown in
'her face goes still, remote, unreflecting. It's as if she's not inside it'
(p. 221) will be developed in Elaine's paintings of her.

greenhouse effect Elaine's father is ahead of his time in predicting the
'greenhouse effect' where excessive methane emission destroys the ozone
layer around the earth, leading to 'global warming'
Möbius strip invented by August Ferdinand Möbius (1798–1868)
Klein bottle invented by Felix Klein (1849–1925)

IX: LEPROSY

The painting titled *Leprosy* is described on p. 352. The title also connects
with a popular song that Elaine and Cordelia parody in High School
(p. 229).

CHAPTER 41   The retrospective exhibition receives good previews;
              Elaine realises that she may have changed places with
              Cordelia

In the present-tense narrative, Charna telephones Elaine to tell her that good previews of the exhibition have appeared in the 'Entertainment' pages of the newspaper. Elaine hopes that Cordelia will read the review, and describes the 'portrait' of her, *Half a Face*, noting that the title is 'odd' since Cordelia's whole face is actually visible in the painting. Behind the foregrounded image is a second face which is covered in a white cloth (in an echo of Elaine's dream on p. 360). Elaine notes that she had failed to capture Cordelia's eyes as she had wanted, painting them 'frightened' instead of 'strong'. This leads Elaine to realise that she is less afraid of seeing Cordelia again than of the suspicion that she *became* Cordelia when, at some point she cannot specify, they 'changed places'.

An explanation of the title of the painting, *Half a Face*, is indirectly provided on p. 411 in Elaine's theory of 'reflection'.

Throughout the novel, it is clear that the images Elaine produces have almost a 'mind of their own'. In that they are produced by her unconscious mind, this is literally the case. This is very true of the expression, 'But the eyes sabotaged me' (p. 227).

Elaine expresses the idea that she and Cordelia have changed places: signs of this sense of swapped identities have already been provided: the horror-comic story of the twins and the mirror (p. 211), for example, has previously introduced the theme of supernatural merging (see also Prefatory Material).

eclectic borrowing images, **symbols**, or ideas from several different sources
Post-feminist an intellectual position which attempts to update and modify **feminist** analysis. Elaine's complaint about the use of the term here is that it is clichéd and, in addition, inappropriately applied to her work

CHAPTER 42   Elaine reaches puberty; the power-shifts between
              herself and Cordelia

At school, Elaine remains silent and watchful in contrast to the noisy and increasingly chaotic Cordelia. One day, the girls walk home from school in similar weather conditions to those preceding the incident in the ravine (Chapter 35); further, Cordelia and Elaine feel 'elated' as they had before. These similarities alert the reader to the fact that a crucial point in the relationship between the two girls has been reached.

Cordelia falls into the snow (in an echo of the 'snow angel' on p. 185), and Elaine cannot understand why this disturbs her so much. Cordelia introduces Grace Smeath as a topic of conversation and this soon degenerates into vicious abuse of the Smeath family. Sitting in a cemetery, Elaine's mood suddenly darkens and she manages to convince Cordelia that she is a vampire and that she has a twin who takes her place during daytime. Cordelia's nervousness and uncertainty develop into terror and Elaine enjoys her 'malevolent little triumph' which has left her the 'stronger' of the two.

The evil eye mentioned here is associated in particular with Mrs Smeath (where the image converges with the idea of her 'bad heart'), with the cat's eye marble, and with supernatural ways of seeing. To give the 'evil eye' means to curse a person, or to wish them ill, and it is associated with witchcraft in particular.

The 'energy' referred to in 'energy has passed between us' (p. 233) is power and connects with Stephen's theoretical discourse on pp. 219–20. The word 'energy' also suggests a type of electric current and, further, a type of 'demonic' energy.

highball a cocktail
parodies comic versions of songs

CHAPTER 43   **Elaine's 'mean mouth'; Cordelia as 'target practice'; boys, dates, and silences**

Time is moving quickly at this stage of the retrospective narrative. Elaine is now in Grade Eleven and has developed a reputation for possessing a 'mean mouth' which viciously isolates her female victims' weak points. Elaine uses Cordelia for 'target practice'; this is both an exercise and an expression of her new power.

Given Elaine's traumatic history with girls, it is unsurprising that she feels more comfortable in male company, and she has no difficulty in attracting boyfriends. She understands their psychologies and is able to decipher the meaning of their silences. She does not fall in love with any of her boyfriends, and understands that her need for them is based in visual territories. Elaine remains sexually immature, but her painter's 'vision' is developing quickly.

The idea of boundaries, lines, and edges is again registered in expressions like 'the border of the socially acceptable' and 'walking on thin ice' (p. 235).

Stephen's theoretical discourse on the physical properties of matter on p. 220 is recalled here in 'The body is pure energy, solidified light' (p. 240). Similarly, where Elaine had earlier noted that the trick of listening to silences was a form of 'walking through walls' (p. 238), Stephen's belief in the theoretical ability to 'walk through walls' (p. 220) is recalled.

Anschluss annexation of Austria by Germany in 1938

peplum short skirt-like section at the back of a jacket, part of the post-war 'New Look' initiated by Christian Dior

ducktails hairstyle with hair flicked to the back in the shape of a duck's tail

neck slang term for a prolonged kissing session

corsages flower sprays worn on the bodice of a woman's dress; usually sent by a man to the woman he is escorting to a formal occasion

CHAPTER 44   A murder in the ravine; the Earle Grey Players;
             Cordelia's relationship with her father

A girl of Elaine's age-group is found murdered in the ravine; she has been molested, but somehow an aura of shame contaminates the victim rather than the murderer.

Elaine discusses the fact that Cordelia has no idea how to communicate with boys, and notes that her exaggerated 'performances' frighten them away. Continuing the emphasis upon Cordelia as a performer, Elaine remembers that she had participated in a travelling troupe's production of Shakespeare's *Macbeth*. As Props Assistant, Cordelia replaces the rotten cabbage used to represent Macbeth's head in the final scene, not realising that a fresh cabbage will bounce when dropped. This ruins the final moments of the play and Cordelia is deeply troubled by her mistake. Elaine deliberately increases her misery by ruthlessly teasing her about the incident.

Elaine notes that dinners in Cordelia's household are informal and relaxed when her father is absent, but formal and tense when he is present. Where all the members of the family successfully please Cordelia's father, Cordelia herself is unable to do so. Elaine despises her for being so 'abject' in his presence.

Elaine's dreams are becoming increasingly expressive of her psychological state.

Stephen's perceptive observation that 'Cordelia has a tendency to exist' (p. 242) defines Cordelia in her shape-shifting 'tendency' towards absence. This is also a meaning behind the title of Elaine's painting *Half a Face* (p. 227).

Elaine's dreams express the range of her repressed anxieties in **metaphorical** terms: they also express her more general psychological state in that the sealed but forcibly burst purse and the wrapped head suggest a state of extreme repression where something is more safely kept concealed: 'I know that if I do the head will come alive' (p. 250). As such, the head wrapped in the cloth suggests Elaine's own unconscious which must be kept covered in case it 'comes alive'; if it does so, it will force her into remembering aspects of her past that she cannot bear to face.

Macbeth a further reference to this play (see also pp. 112–3)

E=mc2 the general theory of relativity formulated by Albert Einstein (1879–1955)

Earle Grey Players a fictitious travelling theatre troupe, comically named after an English tea

CHAPTER 45   **Elaine catches a glimpse of her past and instantly represses it**

Cordelia tells Elaine that the holes she had dug in the ground as a child were an attempt to create a 'safe' haven where she could be alone. She also states that she had hated Queen Mary's school, and had counted Elaine as her only real friend.

This 'confessional' reminiscence trips Elaine into an unwanted glimpse of her repressed memories of childhood. She feels a sudden 'flush of shame, of guilt and terror', and is aware of feeling disgusted with herself for no reason that she can identify. She instantly closes the door on this glimpse of the past but remaining in her head are images of a square of darkness (the grave), and of purple flowers (Deadly Nightshade).

As a child, Cordelia believed that by remaining invisible and silent – 'I used to think that if I kept very still … I would be safe' (p. 252) – she would be able to avoid incurring her father's displeasure (there may also be a suggestion that she is a victim of incestuous abuse here). The pressure this has imposed upon Cordelia is at the root of her troubled psyche (see also Chapter 54).

'There is that glimpse, during which I can see' (p. 253): Elaine's flashback to childhood is described in terms of physical vision. 'Insight' and 'sight' are profoundly connected in this novel: refusing 'insight' at this stage of the narrative, Elaine is **metaphorically** 'blind'.

CHAPTER 46   Cordelia disintegrates; Elaine finds her vocation

Without knowing the reason why, Elaine begins to avoid Cordelia whose schoolwork and personal appearance are disintegrating. Finally, she and her family move away. Elaine sits her Grade Thirteen exams and, in the middle of her Biology papers, realises that she will become a painter.

Cordelia contacts Elaine one day and asks her to visit her. Cordelia seems to have suffered some kind of breakdown, and Elaine is shocked by her appearance and manner. The only thing that Cordelia is interested in doing is reliving her past which she has mythologised as a 'golden age'. Elaine panics in case Cordelia begins to journey further back into their relationship (thus triggering unwanted memories), and she hardens against her in self-protection. She makes a hurried exit and admits that she is 'dismayed. . . by my cruelty and indifference'.

In connecting with Elaine, it is as if Cordelia can reconnect with herself: 'some connection to her old life, or to herself' (p. 259). Since their identities are so entwined, Cordelia may feel that only when she is in contact with Elaine can she be 'whole'. As we can see in the present-tense narrative, the same also appears to be true of Elaine who feels incomplete without Cordelia.

raceme, rhizome botanical terms; the first refers to stems producing flowers at the top, and the second refers to stems that grow underground with roots and leaves branching off them

photosynthesis process by which plants convert carbon into tissue using sunlight and releasing oxygen

Scrofulariaciae monopetal plants

legumes deriving from the French *légume*, generic name for beans, peas, and so on

X: LIFE DRAWING

The painting *Life Drawing* is described between pp. 365–6. The title *Life Drawing* refers to the exercise that the painting depicts (painting nudes): it also refers to the fact that, from this point forward in the narrative, Elaine's unconscious project is to 'draw' her 'life'.

CHAPTER 47   Diseases of the memory, and Elaine's lunch with Jon

The present-tense narrative resumes with Elaine considering diseases of the memory. She again thinks that she sees Cordelia, and considers the idea that Cordelia's name may have affected her psychologically: in Shakespeare's *King Lear*, Cordelia was the 'rejected' sister 'who was not heard'.

The restaurant in which Elaine meets Jon **symbolises** the changes that have occurred in Toronto in her absence. Jon seems to have reached a level of self-perception which had previously been absent, but Elaine feels that this may only be a 'performance'. Nevertheless, she reflects that she finds it a great deal easier to forgive men than women.

Having left Jon after lunch, Elaine considers her painting, *Falling Women*. This painting and the associations it generates will trigger the subsequent narrative relating to Elaine's relationships with Josef and Jon.

The opening line, 'There are several diseases of the memory' obviously connects with Elaine's radical repression of her two-year period of childhood trauma.

'A lot of my paintings then began in my confusion about words', Elaine says (p. 268). The title *Falling Women* is a **malapropism** (a comic verbal confusion); the correct term is 'fallen women', a Victorian term for prostitutes or for any woman who had 'fallen' into sinfulness. In the painting, the idea has been made literal in that women are shown falling from a bridge, and this suggests Elaine's childish habit of converting abstract ideas into literal images.

hatchet-job an interview or article which deliberately undermines the subject

CHAPTER 48   Elaine at her first 'life-class'

The **retrospective** narrative is rejoined at a later stage in Elaine's life; she has graduated from High School and is now studying Art and Archaeology at Toronto University. However, something has compelled her to take night classes in art, and this chapter opens on Elaine drawing her first female nude. She is perturbed by the extensive flesh of the model and has no desire to imagine feeling her body in order to capture its 'tactile' nature on canvas as her tutor advises.

The class is taught by a European refugee, Josef Hrbik, another 'displaced person' in the novel (see p. 281). Elaine shows him her portfolio in order to gain entry into the class; she had only begun painting the previous summer and has little material, but he admits her anyway since he is intrigued to see 'what we can make of you'.

It is hardly surprising that Hrbik's eyes are the first thing Elaine notices about him given the obsession with eyes, vision, and various forms of sight throughout the novel.

Hrbik's question to Elaine, 'Why do you want to learn?' and her reply, 'I don't know' provide an echo of the journalist's question to Elaine, and of her answer, on p. 91. On both occasions, Elaine has no honest answer to give since she genuinely has no idea why she needs to paint.

Moonlight Sonata popular name for Opus 27, No. 2 by Ludwig van
Beethoven (1770–1827)
Muskoka a holiday resort north of Toronto

CHAPTER 49   Elaine's college life and her growing allegiance to art
through which she 'lets herself go'

Elaine views slides of various Classical sculptings in her Art and
Archaeology classes. The artefacts interest her but she is disconcerted
by the literal disembodiment of the mutilated statues.

Elaine describes the conformist student body with which she at first
tries to 'blend in'; the majority of the students on her course are girls who
are simply 'marking time' before marriage. Elaine makes it clear that her
true allegiance is to art which she has now recognised as her 'lifeline, my
real life'. Gradually, she metamorphoses into an 'arty beatnik', and wears
the austere, black clothing of her classmates. Her new identity is disliked
by Mrs Finestein who decides that she is 'letting herself go'.

The surface meaning of this **idiomatic** expression, 'letting herself
go', indicates a shameful carelessness in terms of personal appearance
(usually applied to women). However, a second, more crucial
meaning is also available since it is only in painting, her 'lifeline',
that Elaine is able to 'let go' of her unconscious pain. All the
idiomatic phrases in this novel are similarly flexible in their
connotations.

CHAPTER 50   Elaine as 'one of the boys'; Susie is introduced and
Jon is reintroduced

The cultural history of Toronto is developed in Elaine's memories of
drinking with the 'boys' from her life-class. The bars they frequent are
segregated in an echo of the illogical gender division at Queen Mary's
School. Elaine enjoys being treated as 'one of the boys', and listens
unperturbed to her classmates' derisive comments about 'lady painters'.
Far from being offended by this talk, she relishes the feeling that she is
siding with men against women.

Elaine's status as sole female in the group of men is threatened
when another female classmate, Susie, joins the group one night. She

is conventionally pretty and blonde, and she defends Josef Hrbik against the boys' attack. Hrbik's history as a postwar 'displaced person' is given.

Elaine is so alienated from her emotions that most of the time she seems to drift through life on 'automatic pilot': 'It seems to have arrived fully formed, out of nowhere' (p. 279).

The term '*displaced person*' refers to refugees admitted to Canada on political asylum, but it is also used throughout the novel to refer to any character suffering from a profound sense of alienation or unbelonging. Characters such as Victor Banerji, Mrs Finestein, Hrbik and Elaine each 'stand out' from their environment or group and are marked as 'different'. In failing to belong to a 'place', they are 'displaced'.

Uncle Joe nickname given to Josef Stalin, Soviet dictator, who died in 1953
Hungarian Revolution 1956, when Hungarian independence was crushed by the Soviets

CHAPTER 51   Elaine decides that Hbrik needs 'rescuing' from Susie

Elaine's 'real life' takes place at nighttime when she attends life-class, but in her 'surface' life, it is February and the Art and Archaeology course has reached the Renaissance period. Elaine is confronted with numerous images of the Virgin Mary which fall into various categories.

At life-class, Elaine observes Susie closely, just as Cordelia had once observed her. Elaine realises that Susie is having an affair with Hrbik, though she immediately casts Hrbik as Susie's '*besotted*' victim. The older women in the class sympathise with Susie, but Elaine decides to rescue Hrbik from her clutches. She has not yet realised that it is Susie who is the one in need of 'protection'.

The phrase 'speeding through the Renaissance' (p. 283) **parodies** the pace with which subjects of study are routinely 'covered' in courses, but also connects with Stephen's point that time can run 'faster in some places than in others' (p. 219).

'Susie herself is incapable of love, she's too shallow' (p. 285): Elaine's harsh judgements against women continue to be delivered automatically, and derive from her longstanding distrust of women.

reliquaries case or shrine for holy relics

CHAPTER 52   Elaine at home in the cellar; Stephen's arrest

Elaine has now moved into the family cellar which she has decorated with theatre posters and with her numerous drawings of feet (she had once mutilated her own). Her father continues to lecture her about recent scientific developments, but Elaine is now uninterested and uninformed. Victor Banerji has returned to India having apparently been a victim of racism in Canada.

Stephen is now a postgraduate at the University of California where he is working on 'The Nature of the Universe'. One day, he accidentally trespasses on a military testing zone and is arrested as a spy. His tutor has to bail him out. He writes to Elaine, talking to her as though she were still a child, and she realises that he has no idea who he is writing to since 'I have surely changed beyond all recognition' (p. 291). She worries for Stephen because she knows that being 'out in the open, and surrounded by strangers' is more dangerous than he realises.

The chain of negatives 'I do not realize … I have not heard … I do not know' (p. 288) contributes to the sense that Elaine is becoming increasingly detached from the 'daytime' world. In addition, her 'lack of appetite and pallor' and her sleeplessness suggest an almost vampiric existence.

Waiting for Godot is an **existentialist** play by Samuel Beckett (1906–89) first performed in Paris in 1953. The play involves two characters who wait for a being named 'Godot' to arrive; he never does so and remains absent so that their wait is futile. This is echoed in Elaine's equally futile 'wait' for the appearance of the absent Cordelia in Elaine's present-tense narrative.

No Exit (*Huis Clos*) is a play by Jean-Paul Sartre (1905–80), one of the leading existentialist philosophers. *No Exit* was first performed in Paris in 1944 and has also been translated as *In Camera*. The play involves a group of people who have recently died; they recall their experiences on earth and reach the conclusion that people create their own hell in others. This directly connects with Elaine's relationship with Cordelia.

'botanist manqué' an unfulfilled, or would-be, botanist

CHAPTER 53   Elaine's affair with Josef Hrbik begins

Elaine recalls the beginning of her affair with Josef. He continues to see Susie who wants to marry him and who is clearly becoming increasingly desperate. Meanwhile, Elaine moves out of home, takes a summer job in a restaurant, and continues to sleep with Josef throughout the summer. She notes that she is 'in love with his need', and listens to his disturbed dreams which are products of his 'baleful' wartime memories. These dreams include images of women whose faces are obscured in a variety of ways. Elaine realises that she feels 'ancient', despite her youth. Finally, in the middle of the French meal which begins the chapter, it occurs to Elaine that she is deeply unhappy.

> Together with his bad dreams, Josef's mental trauma is similar to Elaine's: 'He says these things are too disturbing for him and he wants only to forget them' (p. 298). However, Elaine is a still more extreme case since she refuses even to acknowledge that there are incidents in the past that she needs to 'forget'.

> Josef's dreams involve obliterating female identity: 'He dreams of a woman wrapped up in cellophane, even over her face' (p. 298). This possibly accounts for his attraction to Elaine who has obliterated her own identity to the extent that she has become a 'blank canvas'.

CHAPTER 54   Elaine meets Cordelia again, and meets her own
              reflection in Cordelia's mirrored sunglasses

Elaine agrees to meet Cordelia who is now a bit-part player with Tyrone Guthrie's Stratford Shakespearean Festival. She talks about her work and mentions that she longs to play the First Witch in *Macbeth*.

Cordelia starts reminiscing, and remembers enjoying shoplifting because 'It was something I could have' (p. 303); this recalls her earlier statement that the hole she dug in the garden was an attempt to create 'some place that was all mine' (p. 252). Following this 'confession', Cordelia immediately seeks refuge behind a pair of mirrored sunglasses, and Elaine feels diminished in their reflection.

Cordelia gives Elaine tickets to attend a performance of *The Tempest* in which she appears as an 'airy spirit'. Elaine looks closely, but cannot determine which of the figures on the stage is Cordelia.

The significance of the lines *'Then if you speak ...'*, from Shakespeare's *Measure for Measure*, I.4.12–13, is registered in Cordelia's 'shorthand' method of remembering them. Her summary, 'Speak, hide face, show face, shut up', recalls her 'confession' in Chapter 45 when she had noted that if she remained motionless, silent and invisible, she would be 'safe' from her father.

Since it is considered unlucky for actors to mention the title *Macbeth*, Cordelia rather pretentiously refers to the play as '*The Tartans*'. This reintroduces the play into the novel.

Cordelia may resort to her mirrored sunglasses as a form of self-protection (she has just 'confessed' to Elaine), or perhaps as a means of turning Elaine's critical gaze back on herself (see also the idea of 'reflection', p. 411). Whichever accounts for the action (and both are likely to be involved), Elaine is certainly psychologically disorientated by it: 'in duplicate and monochrome and a great deal smaller than life-size' (p. 303). The fact that the sunglasses are mirrored continues a chain of references throughout the novel connecting Cordelia with various mirrors.

'But I can't tell' see also p. 127
Stratford Shakespearean Festival founded at Stratford-on-Avon, Ontario, during the 1950s by Sir Tyrone Guthrie (1900–71)

CHAPTER 55   **Josef reshapes Elaine in the oppressive summer heat; Elaine and Jon make love for the first time**

Josef and Elaine drink cocktails, and Josef reveals that he has once shot a man. He tells Elaine that he loathes Canada and will leave for America and a career in film direction at the first opportunity. He asks Elaine

whether she would 'do anything' for him, and is unsurprised when she
says that she would not: she, however, is astonished by her own, 'truthful'
response.

Josef continues to see Susie. Elaine is made uneasy by the idea that
they may discuss her because she would have no control over that
situation. Whilst she is working in the Swiss Chalet one day, Jon appears;
this is the first time that Elaine has ever seen him during the day. He asks
her to go out for a drink with him, and when they later leave the Maple
Leaf bar together, Elaine begins to cry, though she has no idea why. Jon
takes her back to his apartment, and they make love.

> Josef's 'rearrangement' of Elaine suggests the extent to which she is
> a 'blank canvas', capable of being reshaped into any image: 'You
> look like a marvellous gypsy' (p. 309).

> Elaine clearly has no idea what is in her own mind. Her tactless, but
> honest, response to Josef's question, 'This is a surprise to me … It
> sounds rude' (p. 305) amazes her because she had not realised how
> she had felt until she has spoken. Similarly, her tears upon leaving
> the bar seem unaccountable to her, and are also the result of
> unconscious tensions which her conscious fails to register.

Manhattans a cocktail mixture consisting of whiskey and vermouth

XI: FALLING WOMEN

The painting of this title has been described on p. 268. On p. 412, an
admirer of the painting interprets it in **feminist** terms but, as Elaine has
explained on p. 268, the men in the painting act without 'volition' and are
as blameless in the 'downfall' of the women as are the women themselves
(p. 268).

CHAPTER 56   **The present-tense narrative traces the changing face
of Toronto; a middle-Eastern refugee**

Back in the present-tense narrative, Elaine is a little drunk following her
'retrospective' lunch with Jon. She wanders through the Toronto streets
and regards the sophisticated shops which have arisen on the site of

Josef's old 'semi-hovel'. Thinking about Josef, Elaine feels that she is able to appraise him accurately now that time has given her 'perspective'.

Feeling a touch on her arm, Elaine expects to see Cordelia. However, it is a Middle-Eastern woman, another 'displaced person', who is the homeless victim of an unspecified war. Elaine tells us that this is the war that killed Stephen, though this section of the narrative has not yet been encountered (see Chapter 68). Elaine, ever the 'bleeding heart', gives the woman money, and feels overwhelmed by an awareness of *'need, need, help, help'* all around her.

'This is the war that killed Stephen' (p. 314) is foreshadowing a narrative event yet to occur. Not only does this encourage the reader to read on, but it also contributes to the sense of coexistent tenses in a novel where echoes of the future consistently recur.

puttees strips of cloth wound around the calf; associated with British Army uniform in the South African War and the First World War (1914–18)
South African War fought between Britain and the Boers (1899–1902)
wimple a stiff headdress, associated with nuns
Allah Islamic name for God

CHAPTER 57   Susie's illegal abortion; Elaine rejects Josef

Elaine is now in relationships with both Jon and Josef. She continues to avoid Susie, but responds to an emergency telephone call from her. When she arrives at Susie's apartment, she finds Susie semi-conscious and bleeding heavily following an illegal abortion. Half of her realises that Susie is not the sly manipulator she had thought her to be but, even so, a 'small, mean voice' inside her head says, *'It serves her right'* (p. 321).

Susie rejects Josef who sinks into guilty self-pity; Elaine also rejects Josef because she begins to dislike his weakness. Subsequently, Elaine has a dream in which the image of Susie is transposed onto that of the childish Carol who spitefully asks, 'Don't you know what a twin set is?' (p. 323). The feelings of self-loathing that this triggers in Elaine alert her to the fact she has behaved badly.

'Something has changed in her, hardened' (p. 321) recalls Elaine's statement following her rejection of the girls: 'There's something hard in me, crystalline, a kernel of glass' (p. 193).

'It's like being able to make people appear and vanish' (p. 322) is what Elaine had managed to do with her persecutors as a child. However, the 'vanishing act' is an illusion only as Elaine could not make her childhood tormentors, and the traumas they inflicted, 'vanish' from her unconscious mind. In the same way, causing Josef to 'vanish' at this point in the narrative does not prevent unsettling, guilt-inducing dreams about Susie and, by extension, about Josef.

knitting needle sometimes used in 'backstreet' abortions to terminate pregnancy. Abortion was illegal at this time

CHAPTER 58 **Elaine's relationship with Jon develops; Elaine becomes fascinated with painting light-reflecting surfaces, and embarks on a course in Advertising Art**

With Josef dismissed from her life, Elaine concentrates fully on her relationship with Jon who begins to paint Abstract paintings which 'make your eyes hurt'.

The Art and Archaeology course continues its romp through the centuries. In her art, Elaine rejects oil-painting and experiments instead with egg tempera, an early Renaissance technique; she also becomes particularly drawn to Jan Van Eyck's painting, '*The Arnolfini Marriage*'.

Elaine embarks on a new night course in Advertising Art, hoping that it will lead to employment following her studies. Jon mocks the course because he disapproves of art that recreates 'real' objects.

The painting of '*The Arnolfini Marriage*' by Johannes Van Eyck, 1390–1441, shows a man and a woman in the foreground: their images are reflected in a convex mirror that hangs on a wall behind them. However, a third image can also be identified in the mirror, despite the fact that no third figure can be seen in the foregrounded painting (this should be compared with Elaine's dream-experience on p. 250). As such, this hidden figure connects with Elaine's sense that Cordelia is a menacing presence lurking unseen on stage or in the street. The convex glass of the mirror also suggests an eye, and this sustains the chain of references to 'sight', 'insight' and 'vision'.

egg tempera, gesso early Renaissance method of painting using egg yolk. Gesso is a type of plaster which is used to provide an absorbent base

Norman Rockwell popular American illustrator (1894–1978), renowned for his clichéd images of white, middle-class families

CHAPTER 59 **Elaine graduates and lands her first job; she attends Stephen's lecture on the 'First Picoseconds'**

Elaine metamorphoses from an art student into a career-woman and moves into her first apartment. Jon teases her about its rudimentary homeliness, but he secretly finds the comfort enticing. Elaine's father has left Toronto University and has returned to field research; her parents have sold their house and moved North.

Elaine attends a lecture that Stephen is giving at Toronto University and is astonished by his transformed appearance. His paper is largely unintelligible to her, but she learns that there are 'a great many more dimensions than four' (p. 332). Afterwards, they swap reminiscences of their childhood, and Elaine is surprised that she is able to remember events that Stephen cannot recall. This alerts her to the fact that if he has forgotten certain things, then she must have forgotten some events herself. She is already aware that there are two years 'missing' from her memories of him.

The relevance of Stephen's lecture (pp. 331–2) to Elaine's story is indicated on more than one level. First, Elaine has no idea of the 'energies' that have shaped her psyche; secondly, the 'forces' that have engulfed her in the form of the traumas inflicted by Cordelia and the girls will become 'distorted' into the **figural** language of the later paintings until they are beyond 'recognition'. All she has at this stage of the retrospective narrative are 'fragments of the past'.

particle accelerator a scientific laboratory used in nuclear physics
Picoseconds fractional units of times
Munchkins elves in *The Wonderful Wizard of Oz* (L. Frank Baum, 1856–1919)
Unified Field Theory combining quantum theory and Einstein's general theory of relativity (see Chapter 44)
fiat lux (Latin) 'Let there be light', God's words upon the creation of the world, Genesis 1:3

CHAPTER 60   Elaine falls accidentally pregnant, and her repressed
memories begin to return

When Elaine falls accidentally pregnant, her psychological health
is threatened and she becomes disturbed by bad dreams. In addition,
she begins to paint images of her childhood, and is aware that the
domestic items she paints are 'suffused with anxiety' of a type that she
cannot define. Particularly disturbing are the several images of Mrs
Smeath that Elaine compulsively produces. Panicked by the unplanned
pregnancy, and haunted with fears of Jon's potential desertion of her,
Elaine's unconscious mind 'codes' into her paintings repressed memories
connected with her childhood sense of shame, guilt and fear.

Elaine interprets her feelings of 'void' in terms of images derived
from Stephen's theoretical discourse: 'I feel as if I'm at the centre
of nothingness ... that I'm exploding slowly outwards, into the
burning cold void of space' (p. 336). Here, she feels like a type of
'black hole', empty of sensation and materiality.

'Whatever has happened to me is my own fault' (p. 338) connects
with the spiteful phrase of dismissal and judgement, 'It serves her
right', which has occurred earlier in Elaine's reaction to Susie's
predicament.

CHAPTER 61   Jon and Elaine's married life; Elaine attends a
women's meeting

Following Chapter 60, there has been a time-lapse of three years. Elaine
describes the progress of her life in the intervening period. A period of
'fogginess' followed the birth of Sarah, Elaine's eldest daughter, but
Elaine now feels more energised. However, her life with Jon, whom she
married, is difficult, and they have begun to fight. Unable to assert herself
verbally, Elaine resorts to 'different arts' in expressing her anger such as
shrugs and 'silent' rebukes.

Elaine attends a women's meeting; this is clearly an 'encounter'
group produced by the nascent 'second wave' feminist movement that was
beginning to make its mark on North America at this time (mid-to-late
1960s). Elaine feels liberated by the attitudes she hears expressed, yet
feels uneasy and vulnerable in the company of women. At the end of the

chapter, Elaine describes her painting of the Virgin Mary which depicts *Our Lady of Perpetual Help* as a lioness.

Elaine attributes a postnatal sense of fuzziness – 'I felt clogged, as if swimming with my clothes on' (p. 342) – to hormonal activity. However, the time lapse between Chapter 60 and Chapter 61 also suggests that the feelings of guilt and shame she described at the end of Chapter 60, together with the fact that she has been wrenched from girlhood into a confrontation with her own gynaecology (which had disgusted her as a child), may account for this sense of being 'clogged' more than hormonal overload.

At the end of the chapter, Elaine finally discovers an assertive voice: 'I'm mad because you're an asshole'. It seems as though the 'anger' expressed in the women's meeting may have had more of a direct effect upon her than she realised.

CHAPTER 62   **The women's art exhibition; an ink-attack**

Together with three other artists from the women's group, Elaine participates in a women's art exhibition. Elaine describes the **feminist** work of her fellow artists and feels her own paintings to be 'too merely pretty' in comparison.

On the opening night, Elaine surveys and describes the Mrs Smeath series of paintings: she declares that 'It's still a mystery to me, why I hate her so much' (p. 352). A religious fanatic storms into the exhibition and proceeds to deface Elaine's painting, *White Gift*, with a bottle of ink. The newspaper that reports the incident uses the patronising, sneering headline, 'FEATHERS FLY AT FEMINIST FRACAS'.

Jody's art is a comment upon the way in which the female body is exploited for male benefit – 'Jody does store mannequins, sawn apart' (p. 347) – and is thus a feminist statement. The wrecked mannequins also sustain the theme of disembodiment as throughout.

dying turtle see Chapter 32

CHAPTER 63   **Elaine visits Cordelia at a private 'rest home'**

Following a failed suicide attempt, Cordelia's family has institutionalised her. It is several years since Elaine last saw Cordelia, and she is physically much changed. Cordelia tells Elaine about her suicide attempt and asks Elaine to help her escape from the home. When Elaine refuses, Cordelia asserts that Elaine has always hated her, but this surprises Elaine who has no memory of ever having hated Cordelia.

Three months later, Elaine writes Cordelia an evasive letter, but the letter is returned with '*address unknown*' on the envelope. Cordelia has found her own way of escaping from the home. Elaine experiences the same sense of unease as she had when trying to spot Cordelia on stage: Cordelia is 'out there', lurking unseen.

Elaine has a series of disturbing dreams about Cordelia. If Elaine was not 'totally glued together' before seeing Cordelia again, the sense of guilt and shame she experiences upon deserting Cordelia for the second time serves only to 'unglue' her further.

> 'You aren't any crazier than I am' (p. 358): since Elaine is suffering from paralysing repression, since this gives rise to 'haunted' dreams, visions and paintings, and since she will herself attempt suicide later in the narrative, her statement here is unwittingly **ironic**

XII: ONE WING

The painting of this title is described on p. 407: painted after Stephen's death, it is a triptych (in three panels), and its title derives from a song that Stephen and Elaine had sung as children (see p. 24).

CHAPTER 64   **A 1940s diner; *Life Drawing*; Jon and Elaine make love for the last time**

In the present-tense narrative, Elaine sits in a restaurant that has been 'themed' as a 1940s-style diner. Elaine considers that all the relics of the past will one day become 'fashionable' again (as on p. 3, 'Nothing goes away').

Elaine then wanders the Toronto streets and finds Josef's old house. Elaine recalls seeing a film that was probably directed by Josef; the film 'coded' the triangular relationship between himself, Elaine and Susie. Elaine herself has told her 'version' of the story in the painting *Life Drawing*, which she describes on pp. 365–6.

Towards evening, Elaine meets Jon for the second time that day. They eventually return to Jon's apartment and make love. Elaine does not see this as a betrayal of Ben because her relationship with Jon belongs to a set of feelings, and to a 'space' and 'time', that 'pre-date' him.

The emphasis upon 'dimensions' persists – 'a universe of two dimensions' (p. 366) – thus connecting with Stephen's theoretical discourse. This chapter also begins with the description of the '4–D's Diner', a pun relying on sound (in a North American accent, 'forties' would sound like 'four-dees'), and upon the meaning of a four-dimensional universe (with time as the fourth dimension, as on p. 219). This is appropriate given that this is a 'retrospective' 1940s-style diner.

zucchini courgettes

Pre-Raphaelite an aesthetic movement associated with Gabriel Dante Rossetti (1828–82) in particular

spritzers a mixture of white wine and mineral water or soda-water

Regency in the style of early nineteenth-century furniture

diminuendo this refers to a gradual 'falling'. It is the opposite of 'crescendo' (a peak)

CHAPTER 65   **Encouraged by the voice of the absent Cordelia, Elaine attempts suicide as her marriage to Jon deteriorates**

Elaine's relationship with Jon in the 'present-tense' narrative here flows into her deteriorating marriage to Jon in the retrospective narrative. Their crumbling relationship is marked by a type of guerrilla warfare conducted in silence.

As winter sets in, Elaine becomes aware that her head feels 'clogged and cottony', as it had following the birth of Sarah. When Jon does not come home one night, Elaine's despair deepens and she thinks that she can hear a voice inside her head ordering: '*Do it. Come on. Do it*'. Obeying the voice, she cuts her left wrist. Jon finds her and rushes her to hospital. She pretends that her injury was accidental and, though the hospital is suspicious and gently suggests that she consult a psychiatrist, she is released. Elaine knows that the voice was not real, but she also knows that she had heard it, and that it was the excited voice of a nine-year-old child.

A reference to the transgression of boundaries can be detected in 'I've gone too far' (p. 371).

'*Do it. Come on. Do it*' (p. 373) is a direct echo of Cordelia's voice on p. 155. The disembodied voice is connected to Elaine's sense of guilt in abandoning Cordelia twice. It is almost as though Elaine is seeking to make amends with her 'twin' in attempting suicide as she had done.

Exacto knife brand name for a sharp knife which uses replaceable blades

shrink slang for psychiatrist

CHAPTER 66   **Elaine flees Toronto and her marriage to Jon. She resettles in Vancouver where she meets and eventually marries Ben**

Following her suicide bid, Elaine realises that she has to escape Toronto. Jon knows that he can do nothing to prevent her, and Elaine and Sarah relocate to Vancouver.

After a while, Elaine consults a psychiatrist because she feels off 'balance', but the psychiatrist fails to realise that it was what happened to Elaine *after* the age of six that was significant, and not what happened before as he maintains.

Elaine becomes familiar with a group of women artists who are all committed feminists. She becomes aware of resenting these women, partly because she feels 'nervous' about their 'hard, legitimate' judgements. Her hostility in this section results from her sense of vulnerability in the company of women.

Jon and Elaine divorce and, after a series of affairs, Elaine meets and marries Ben. Their relationship is not passionate, but content, and they have a second daughter together. Walking on the seashore, Elaine looks at the mountains and realises that Toronto lies beyond. She cannot even bear to think of the city.

Elaine's traumatised psyche has always been expressed through her hands: 'Gradually I grow back, into my hands' (p. 377). As a child, she had mutilated them; as an adult, at times of intense stress, she cannot paint with them. Here she is indicating that, as her anxiety retreats, she becomes able to use her hands to paint again.

'Confession is popular ... *Don't boss me around*' (pp. 378–9): this section is central to an understanding of Elaine's relationship with women.

Elaine talks of Toronto as 'burning in thought like Gomorrah. At which I dare not look' (p. 382): Gomorrah was one of the cities of the plain destroyed by God in Genesis 18–19. Lot's wife had looked back upon it and had been turned into a pillar of salt. Elaine 'dares not look' back at Toronto because she fears the memories which haunt it.

XIII: PICOSECONDS

The painting titled *Picoseconds* is described on p. 405. The title connects with the minuscule fractions of time discussed in Stephen's lecture (p. 331). Her reference to Bruegel's Icarus creates a parallel with Stephen (who is not represented in the painting) since they were both shot down to earth. The reference also suggests that Stephen's death was predestined even at the time represented in the painting: as always, in this novel, tenses coexist so that echoes of the future are contained in the past.

CHAPTER 67   On the day of the retrospective exhibition opening, Elaine 'kills time' and returns to her childhood streets on Hallowe'en

Elaine eats breakfast the morning after she has slept with Jon. She feels that she has bestowed a type of valediction upon him and upon their relationship. Elaine then takes the subway to her childhood neighbourhood. On the way, she considers how easy it would be for her to 'slip over some ill-defined edge' (p. 386) and become a 'bag lady' (a homeless and thus 'displaced' old woman): in her case, she would not be collecting 'shreds' of 'space' but 'shreds' of 'time'.

    Elaine looks around the streets of her childhood and recalls Cordelia's snow-angel. It is Hallowe'en and Elaine notes that the festival is more extravagantly and colourfully celebrated in Mexico. She decides that North American society has 'rejected that easy flow between dimensions' (p. 387) – the living and the dead – and that our 'ghosts' are 'harder to hear' in consequence.

All Souls' Eve (Hallowe'en) recalls the events of Chapter 20. In addition, if Elaine is to find the witchlike Cordelia, Hallowe'en is perhaps the night on which she could most expect success.

CHAPTER 68   Stephen's murder, five years previously

Elaine supplies details of her brother's death which are based on both 'facts' and on her own imaginative reconstruction of events. Stephen had been on an aeroplane which had been hijacked by Arab terrorists. For some contingent reason, the hijackers had selected Stephen to murder. Elaine recalls that she had not 'made a spectacle' of herself when faced with Stephen's death, but had characteristically detached herself from the tragedy. Considering these events in later years, Elaine's thoughts revolve around the idea of the 'space twin' from p. 219. She realises that she will become older as time passes whereas Stephen will not.

'He died of an eye for an eye [...] too much justice' (p. 388): the brutality of the Biblical injunction, 'an eye for an eye' is associated with Mrs Smeath's ferocious brand of Christianity throughout the novel (see, for example, the painting AN·EYE·FOR·AN·EYE, p. 352). The phrase derives from the Bible, Exodus (21:24), and connotes vicious judgement of the type favoured by Mrs Smeath. The injunction also centralises the theme of sight and vision in this novel (see p. 405, 'An eye for an eye only leads to more blindness').

On one level, her statement that 'The universe is hard to pin down ...' (p. 388) refers to Heisenberg's uncertainty principle which states that scientific observation alters the status of the thing observed. On a second level, it also connects with the nature of vision (and 'point of view') in relation to Elaine's art; as she will discover in Chapter 71, her paintings 'change' when she looks at them with fresh 'insight'. Like the universe, her paintings therefore resist 'being known' (p. 388).

The sense of 'time' as a dimension is indicated in the phrase 'enters the past' (p. 391). 'Pretended flight' (p. 392) connects with the idea of 'lost flight' on p. 131.

ptomaine poisonous alkaloids found in decaying matter

CHAPTER 69   **Elaine's repressed memories return as she finds the cat's eye marble and sees 'her life entire'**

Soon after Stephen's death, Elaine's father dies; her mother will also die a year later. During her last visit to her mother, Elaine listens to her memories of Stephen and Elaine's childhood. Apparently seeking 'forgiveness' from her daughter, she talks of the day that Elaine almost froze to death in the ravine. Flashes of memory begin to pierce Elaine's consciousness.

Elaine and her mother clear out the cellar. They find the old trunk, which Elaine connects with a 'mysterious' 'repository of treasure', and together they sort through the relics of the past. As memories are retrieved, Elaine becomes aware of resenting her mother's helplessness during her 'bad time'. Finally, Elaine discovers her old red bag, looks inside it, and finds the cat's eye marble. Her memories return in a flash.

When Elaine looks into the marble's layers of coloured glass, it is as if she is looking into a reverse crystal ball: 'I look into it, and see my life entire' (p. 398). What she sees is not a vision of the future, but a vision of all the images, experiences and emotions of her past.

sepia-coloured the faded brown of old photographs

CHAPTER 70   **Elaine pleads with the absent Cordelia to release her**

In the present-tense narrative, Elaine walks the streets expecting to find her old school. She finds instead that it has been replaced with a new, 'glossy' building, and she reacts to this erasure as if she has suffered a physical blow. Elaine walks to the eroded hill and stands on the spot where she had stood as a child, listening to the distant playground voices of children. Though it is daytime, she feels as though it is dusk and that 'Ill will surrounds me' (p. 400). She feels the weight of something pushing against her, and silently begs Cordelia to release her from the prison of being forever trapped in her nine-year-old's misery.

XIV: UNIFIED FIELD THEORY

'She's in there somewhere, that other one' (p. 399) connects with the ideas of twinship and of an alien takeover of the body. It also suggests that, though time ages the outward body, a person's identity may actually remain that of a younger version of themselves. This is the sense in which Elaine does not 'want to be nine years old forever' (p. 400).

XIV: UNIFIED FIELD THEORY

The painting of the title is described on p. 408, and is analysed in Textual Analysis, Text 2. The painting's title derives from Stephen's lecture on theoretical physics (p. 331) which creates a tension with the apparently religious nature of the painted subject. Of the images represented in the painting, the bridge, suggesting a boundary and a transitional movement from 'here' to 'there', or from 'then' to 'now', is the most significant at this closing stage of Elaine's story.

CHAPTER 71   **Elaine inspects her efforts to 'preserve' time when she views her paintings before the opening of the retrospective exhibition**

On the opening night of the retrospective exhibition, Elaine arrives at the gallery early and looks at the several paintings of Mrs Smeath. They reveal 'considerable malice', but Elaine is surprised to find that they also reveal a level of compassion which she has never seen in them before. She notes that the injunction, 'An eye for an eye', can only lead to 'more blindness' in a statement that combines the literal with the **metaphorical** 'dimensions'.

Elaine inspects the other paintings, most of which have been encountered earlier in the narrative. *Three Muses*, however, has not yet been encountered, and Elaine describes the images of the three kindly, 'displaced persons' who came to her aid as a child.

Elaine considers whether her paintings have been an attempt to 'preserve' something 'from time'. She feels tempted to destroy the paintings because she can no longer 'control' their meanings which have been transformed in the light of insight. She concludes by noting that she is 'what's left over', meaning that her paintings are the

'dimension' into which all her pain, confusion, and experiences have been transferred.

Elaine's fresh 'sight' – 'for the first time really' (p. 404) – a result of her fresh 'insight' into her life-story, reveals 'dimensions' in the images that she has never 'seen' before. Hence, 'I have said, *Look*. I have said, *I see*' (p. 404). With 'sight' ('*Look*', and '*I see*') comes 'insight' ('*I see*' as in 'I understand'), and vice-versa.

'I can no longer control these paintings' (p. 409) means that Elaine can no longer control her interpretation of them as they are transformed before her eyes. She also means that the visitors to the gallery will, like Charna, impose inaccurate readings upon them, readings over which Elaine will have no 'control'.

Group of Seven members of a Canadian art movement
postmodern an intellectual movement (and critical approach) proceeding Modernism. Postmodernism involves a merging of styles and a refusal of hierarchical judgements regarding them
pastiche consisting of elements from other works or of materials from other forms; connected with postmodernism, it implies both homage and also subversive mockery
Bruegel Pieter Bruegel (*c*.1525–69), Flemish painter known for his highly sophisticated moral commentaries derived from everyday sayings and proverbs. His painting '*The Fall of Icarus*', depicts a youth with man-made wings falling into the sea
frescoes paintings completed on wet plaster
numinous having to do with a deity or presiding spirit
Muses the immortals who inspired the arts in Greek mythology
Jan Gossaert (*c*.1470–1532) a Flemish painter associated with the High Renaissance style and with an over-abundance of detail which art historians connect with *horror vacui* ('fear of emptiness')

CHAPTER 72　　The opening night of the retrospective exhibition; Elaine is crushed when Cordelia fails to appear

Elaine notes that she would not be so terrified of the exhibition opening if the event were being staged in any other city: it is only in Toronto that she feels so vulnerable, or 'scraped naked'.

Elaine hopes that Cordelia will appear at the exhibition party. She no longer needs to ask her about *what* happened in the past (since her memory has returned), but she is driven by a need to ask her *why* it happened. In addition, she feels incomplete without Cordelia's presence, and suggests that Cordelia is similarly incomplete without Elaine's presence: they are like 'twins', 'each of whom has been given half a key' (p. 411). This 'key' refers to entry into the past: each possesses half a key because neither of their 'versions' of their childhood relationship is complete without the other. Until the two are fitted together, there will only be half a story (just as each will only have 'half a face', p. 195).

As the evening wears on, it becomes clear that Cordelia will not appear, and Elaine is crushed when she is forced to acknowledge this. What has annihilated Elaine is the fact that she had been ready for anything except Cordelia's 'absence' and 'silence'.

'She will have her own version' (p. 411): the use of the word 'version' returns attentions to the 'Sub-Versions' name of the gallery and to the chain of meaning implied by it.

'A reflection' (p. 411): this idea connects with Elaine's view of her reflection in Cordelia's mirrored sunglasses (p. 303); that reflection was literally realised, whereas the 'reflection' indicated here is **metaphorical**.

ersatz substitute or imitation

post everything referring to stages following cultural or theoretical movements in which their central ideas are developed, amended and challenged. The prefix 'post' has been added to theories including 'feminism', 'structuralism' and 'modernism'

gangrene the rotting of flesh on a living body

CHAPTER 73   Drunk and tired, Elaine tries to bully the Cordelia who inhabits her into 'dying'

Elaine returns drunk to Jon's studio; she makes coffee and resolves to leave Toronto the next day. She discovers that she is crying, apparently 'without reason', and conducts an inner dialogue with the Cordelia who inhabits and haunts her mind. Using the language of children's shooting games, she tries to bully her 'inner' Cordelia to 'lie down' 'dead'. Drunk and in tears, Elaine cannot lose the 'spectre' of Cordelia.

'Never pray for justice ...' (p. 414): Elaine is here extending her conclusion, 'An eye for an eye leads only to more blindness' (p. 405). Elaine understands that 'justice' can easily slide into 'vengeance'.

'*You're dead, Cordelia*. No I'm not' (p. 414): the italicised words belong to Elaine's inner voice in her silent dialogue with the absent Cordelia. Cordelia's blunt refusal to 'die' suggests the subversive malice of a poltergeist.

XV: BRIDGE

No painting of this title is described in the novel, though it potentially refers to the painting *Unified Field Theory* (p. 408) under another name. Alternatively, it may refer to a painting that has not been described in the novel but which connects with Elaine's dream (p. 145). The title clearly plugs into the emphasis throughout the novel on the bridge over the ravine but, given the fact that this is the final section of the narrative, it is more likely that 'Bridge' refers to a **metaphorical** route from the past and towards the future.

CHAPTER 74   **Elaine returns to the ravine and lays Cordelia's childhood 'ghost' to rest**

The day after the party, Elaine returns to the bridge over the ravine, finally confronting the most traumatic of her memories head-on.

See Textual Analysis, Text 3, where this chapter is discussed.

CHAPTER 75   **Elaine leaves Toronto and, on the plane, realises what she will 'miss'**

Elaine is flying home to Vancouver. Next to her on the plane are two old ladies who behave with teenage abandon. Elaine realises that what she has lost for the future, the prospect of growing old with Cordelia, is what she mourns most.

Looking out over the night sky, Elaine is reminded of Stephen's theories about the stars and the universe (Chapter 19). She converts this theory into a **metaphor** that allows her a way forward into the future. She will survive her history and her trauma because she has enough 'light' in the wake of her Toronto 'retrospective' to 'see by'.

The old ladies' behaviour on the plane – 'red with bravado' (p. 420) – clearly recalls that of Cordelia and Elaine as adolescents (p. 4): the description, 'They're tough as thirteen' directly invites this comparison (p. 420).

There is a connection in the phrase 'shining out of the midst of nothing' (p. 421) with the Bible, John 1:5: 'And the light shineth in darkness; and the darkness comprehended it not' ('comprehended' here means 'enclose and smother'). The word 'nothing' also sustains the emphasis upon voids, vacuums, and states of non-being to the end of the novel.

In the final phrase of the book, 'But it's enough to see by', Elaine refers to both 'light' in which to 'see by' physically, and 'light' (in the 'light' of knowledge) in which to 'see' (as in to 'understand'). Elaine's future remains characterised by a sense of loss, but at least some kind of way forward is perceived by her in the final words of her narrative.

PART THREE

CRITICAL APPROACHES

THEMES

TIME

Like Elaine's painting of her mother, *Cat's Eye* is a novel that is 'drenched in time' (p. 151). Both the Stephen Hawking epigraph and the opening chapter alert the reader to the centrality of this theme in the story that will follow. Grounded in the apparently illogical notion that the future should theoretically be as easily remembered as the past, the novel demonstrates the point that past-tense events condition the nature of present-tense experience and dictate both the events and the experience of the future. In this respect, the three tenses are seen to coexist, and the 'present' and the 'future' become 'sub-versions' of the past.

Because Elaine Risley has ruthlessly repressed the memories of her two-year childhood trauma, she is unable to understand her own emotions and responses in her 'present tense'. The novel deals with her exploration into her past which will lead her to reach an understanding of it: this in turn will produce a way forward into a liveable future. *Cat's Eye* is therefore a novel about survival in three coexistent tenses – past, present and future.

The novel is structured around two time-frames (past and present) which each throw light upon the other. As a result, emphases upon aspects of time and memory abound in a text which is 'retrospective' in all its aspects. To begin with, Elaine's memories of her childhood involve a retrospective journey into the past. Even the present-tense 'Toronto' narrative is marked with the past, because all that Elaine sees around her reminds her of the city's original geography and of events that had occurred within it. As a result, the 'past' is contained in the 'present' since Toronto 'now' constantly reminds her of Toronto 'then'. Toronto represents a 'space' that is inextricably connected with a 'time' in Elaine's life.

Given that the notion of 'space-time' conditions the structure of the narrative, it further conditions the way in which 'time' is felt to be an active force in this novel. 'Time' is perceived as a 'shape, something you could see' (p. 3), and it is therefore constructed as a physical 'dimension' which is as oppressive and disturbing as the 'space' of Toronto itself (the two cannot be separated). In these terms, 'time' becomes for Elaine a tangibly powerful presence, and it operates as an emotional and psychological register of trauma throughout the novel. For example, Elaine's 'live burial' by the girls is felt to be 'a time marker that separates the time before it from the time after' (p. 107). Subsequently, Elaine attempts to evade time: fainting, for example, becomes a means of escaping time since, upon waking, 'Time has gone on without you' (p. 171). At this stage in her life, 'time' has become her enemy.

Numerous additional references to 'time' recur throughout the novel. 'Time' becomes a site of theoretical and metaphysical enquiry, and a series of **idiomatic** expressions ('marking time', 'passing time', 'killing time', and so on). 'Time' also becomes centrally connected with the artist's project, as is made clear when Elaine refers to the artist's task as being to collect 'shreds' of 'time' (p. 386). Similarly, she notes that the images of *Pressure Cooker* were originally an attempt to render her mother 'timeless'. In her work, as in her life, Elaine's world is dominated by a near-physical awareness of 'time' that conditions all her personal and creative perceptions.

Cat's Eye concludes with a tenuous reach towards an indistinct 'future' as Elaine flies away from the 'time' that the 'space' of Toronto represents: her task now is to accommodate her past within a liveable future. The novel therefore begins with a focus upon time as a theoretical construct and concludes with a focus upon time as a lived experience. The theme permeates all that intervenes, so that 'time' can be said to be the determining principle in this 'retrospective' novel where 'Nothing goes away' (p. 3) either in the universe or in the individual psyche.

VISION

Several critics have pointed out that vision is a central theme in *Cat's Eye* where ways of seeing operate as narrative techniques and also as dominant **metaphors** and images. References to sight, seeing, eyes, lenses, and 'visions' constantly alert the reader to this vital theme which is announced in the novel's title.

As a painter, Elaine Risley's 'medium' is vision. All that Elaine sees is recorded in the narrative with the precise attention to visual detail that characterises 'painterly' vision. In addition, the novel emphasises the fact that 'vision' and its opposite, 'blindness', lie at the core of Elaine's story. The narrative involves Elaine's struggle to 'see' her repressed past that is causing her metaphorical 'blindness' in relation to her own story. Only when she looks into the glass of the cat's eye marble does she 'see my life entire' (p. 398) as the scales of ignorance fall from her eyes. With 'sight' (the ability to see her memories), 'insight' follows, and she is able to move towards a position of self-acceptance and forgiveness. This has been the objective of her 'retrospective' visit to Toronto where backwards vision (into the past) is indicated in the very notion of the word 'retrospective' itself.

The theme of 'vision' finds a further echo in the crucial notion of 'visions' as in the case of the vision of the Virgin Mary in the ravine (p. 189). When Elaine finally comes to accept that this 'vision' had not existed other than in her imagination (p. 418), an **irony** relating to the theme of 'sight' becomes clear: Elaine, it seems, is capable of seeing what is not before her eyes but is incapable of seeing what is staring her in the face (as her inability to 'read' her paintings suggests). As a result, 'vision' proves neither stable nor reliable in this novel of various 'visions' and 'revisions' which distort both the events of the past and the experience of the present. Only when Elaine acquires 'insight' into her past will her 'sight' be corrected.

Cat's Eye is a novel of multiple perspectives. These perspectives involve the 'points of view' offered by Elaine's **discursive** and **figural** narratives (see Narrative Techniques), and suggest that alternative 'visions' provide different 'versions' of the same story. In this case, the paintings offer a different version of Elaine's life-story from the one that she has believed to be 'true' ('I am not the sort of girl who has bad times', p. 201). In these terms, the paintings could be defined as Elaine's 'unofficial autobiography', since they provide a 'sub-version' of her history. It is therefore appropriate that the paintings are exhibited at the 'Sub-Versions' gallery: not only do they provide sub-versions of the 'version' of her life that Elaine has thought to be true, but they also radically 'subvert' that account.

The theme of vision is sustained throughout *Cat's Eye* at numerous levels. For example, the narrator peers through several sight-related objects and her narrative is determined by what she sees through them. This narrative manoeuvre can be identified in the **symbol** of the cat's eye marble (see also Metaphors & Imagery). By aligning her sight with that of cat's eye vision, Elaine as a child achieves a sense of emotional detachment. Although this is experienced by the terrified child as a vital protective strategy, its consequences are to remove her from human feeling. She becomes 'blind' to the suffering of others and, armed with cat's eye 'sight', robbed of 'insight' into her own suffering. Only when she rediscovers the marble is this glacial 'vision' reversed, and Elaine rejoins humanity as she reconnects with her memories and emotions.

Additional ideas circulating around sight and vision abound in this novel. Examples include the 'watchful' stars (p. 101) as aligned with the eyes of a judgemental, all-seeing God, the slogan 'There is a Watchbird watching YOU , Cordelia's 'opaque and glinting eyes' (p. 4), the notion of the 'evil eye' (p. 229), the idea of 'reflection' (p. 411), and the emphasis falling upon Cordelia's mirrored sunglasses which force Elaine's gaze back onto herself (p. 303). So numerous are connections with the theme of vision and sight that almost any page of the novel will trigger additional references to ways of seeing whether at the physical, perceptual, or metaphorical level of narrative. *Cat's Eye*, the story of a painter who constructs her past, present, and her future through the 'versions' produced by her multiple 'visions', returns obsessively to the theme of vision and sight at every opportunity.

GOTHIC

As **generic** analyses of this novel have revealed, *Cat's Eye* contains several literary echoes (see Literary Background). Of these, echoes of Gothic literature are particularly dominant.

Associated largely with nineteenth-century writers, Gothic is a narrative form which generates an atmosphere of fear. This usually involves fear of an unnamable, invisible force that lurks on the edge of consciousness. Indeed, the characteristic fear that pervades Gothic fiction is that of something that is assumed to be dead and buried but that shows distinct signs of being neither (see Bram Stoker's *Dracula*, 1897, for example). This is frequently indicated in the key Gothic motif of live burial.

Themes of hiddenness, secrecy and repression 'haunt' Gothic narratives. The atmosphere of repression stems from a central impulse within Gothic literature which is the transgression of the boundary between the conscious and the unconscious realm. Something menacing that is 'buried' in the unconscious mind threatens to break through into the conscious realm, and this gives rise to chains of images relating to the breaking of boundaries or the erosion of borders between separate realms.

It is little wonder that Gothic fiction, with its sense of energies springing from the unconscious and into the conscious mind, has proved so ripe a territory for psychoanalytic criticism, particularly as doubles, split selves, and **doppelgängers** regularly feature within its foreboding plots. Doppelgängers often represent a 'mad twin', a sinister reflection of the central protagonist. In these terms, the **'double'** may be seen as the 'Monstrous Other' that has been produced by the gap between the unconscious and the conscious minds (see, for example, Mary Shelley's *Frankenstein, or The Modern Prometheus*, 1818).

Given these characteristics, it is clear that *Cat's Eye* is a novel that makes extensive use of Gothic impulses. To begin with, the emphasis upon the transgression of boundaries is sustained in the sense that memories of Elaine's two-year period of trauma are constantly on the verge of breaking through from her unconscious and into her conscious mind. To reinforce this idea, references to stepping over an imagined edge or precipice recur throughout the text. Further, in both the 'retrospective' sections dealing with the terrors of Elaine Risley's childhood, and in the 'present-tense' narrative, an atmosphere of fear and menace predominates. As Margaret Atwood notes, '*Cat's Eye* is partly about being haunted' (*Conversations*, p. 237), and Elaine is certainly subject to a permanent fear that 'something' (Cordelia) is 'out there', lurking on the edge of consciousness. Whether on stage as a weasel or an 'airy spirit', whether physically present but 'hidden' behind a 'mask' of performance or behaviour, whether lurking as a shadow in Elaine's mirror, Cordelia is perpetually present but absent at the same time. She can, in fact, be seen as a type of poltergeist, prone to tricks and disappearing acts. Cordelia, with only 'half a face' (p. 227), stalks the border between life and death so perilously that, by the end of the novel, neither we nor Elaine can determine whether she is alive or dead.

In addition, there is recurrent emphasis throughout the text on the idea that Cordelia and Elaine are 'doubles' or 'twins' of some shadowy kind. As the narrator states, 'There is never only one, of anyone' (p. 6), and it is as though the two girls are **metaphorical** doppelgängers where one (apparently Cordelia) is the demonic manifestation of the other (apparently Elaine). However, since, as Elaine remarks, she and Cordelia 'changed places' (p. 227), it is difficult to say with final certainty that the relationship is not, in fact, the other way round.

As the story develops, the reader has the increasing sense that Cordelia and Elaine cannot exist independently of each other, and that only together do they create a 'whole' person (and a 'whole' face). As such, they need each other's reflection to function. Elaine and Cordelia are 'twinned' to such an extent that their meaningful survival depends upon their mutual 'reflections' of each other. This crucial focus upon the idea of reflection introduces another Gothic **motif** into *Cat's Eye*: mirrors and other reflective surfaces. Of particular significance are Cordelia's mirrored sunglasses (p. 303), and the tale of the magic mirror (p. 211) which centralises the Gothic themes of transformation and shape-shifting. Also significant, since it connects several Gothic impulses within the one image, is the convex mirror revealing a lurking, unseen presence in Van Eyck's painting, *The Arnolfini Marriage* (p. 327). Each reinforces the Gothic pulse in this novel and also attests to a sense of symbiosis between Cordelia and Elaine.

Additional Gothic devices can be found in *Cat's Eye* in the motif of 'live burial' (when Elaine is buried in the 'grave', p. 107), the emphasis upon zombies, ghosts and witches (particularly through the horror-story comics and the references to Shakespeare's *Macbeth*), the central repressions, gaps in memory and silences involved in Elaine's psychological condition, and the ravine which potentially symbolises the gulf between the conscious and the unconscious minds. Within a broadly realistic fiction set in present-day Toronto, Atwood weaves a Gothic story of doppelgängers and fear where the shadow of the unconscious transgresses the vulnerable boundaries between dream and waking, and between life and death.

GENDER

Feminist responses to this novel have demonstrated that the linked themes of inter-gender relationships and of gender and society are dominant in *Cat's Eye*. Here, the novelist contests central assumptions of feminist theory, as women are cited as women's primary enemy. At the same time, the restrictions imposed upon women through structures of learned behaviour enforce Simone de Beauvoir's perception that 'one is not born, but rather becomes, a woman' (Beauvoir, *The Second Sex*). This in turn forges connections with the power structures inherent in patriarchal society (based upon 'the law of the father') wherein women are turned into either victims or victimisers in turn.

The theme of gender and society is centralised in the autobiographical story of Elaine Risley. Elaine's early childhood has been spent in wilderness territory in the company of her unconventional family. Her formative years are therefore lived on the edge of mainstream society and in a social unit where gender distinctions do not apply. However, when she settles in Toronto, Elaine is forced to learn gendered rules for the first time. At school, she perceives that boys and girls are separate species as far as society is concerned (as the doors marked 'BOYS' and 'GIRLS' suggest, p. 45), and that different behavioural patterns are expected of them.

Carol Campbell begins Elaine's indoctrination into the rules of gendered behaviour when she teaches Elaine a vocabulary that is unfamiliar to her ('pageboys', 'twin-sets', 'chintz', pp. 47–8). Grace Smeath subsequently introduces Elaine to 'feminine' games (for example, cutting out pictures of consumer goods from a catalogue). Through observation, Elaine learns that it is 'feminine' to pretend inferiority, and 'feminine' not to compete.

This emphasis upon the 'rules' of gender in a patriarchal society subsequently becomes intersected with the theme of inter-gender relationships. Despite the girls' lessons in 'femininity' (and also because of them), Elaine's orientation within the world of women is always tenuous. Her formative relationship with Stephen, and her traumatic experiences at the hands of female persecutors such as Cordelia, Miss Lumley and Mrs Smeath (who cause her to fear her own femaleness) make Elaine the natural ally of men. She is comfortable in their company throughout

High School, does not feel judged by them, and understands their 'silences' (p. 237).

In her relationships with men, Elaine subsequently sets herself in opposition to other women. Though she resents limitations imposed upon her as a result of her gender, she regards siding with men as far preferable to siding with her emotional and psychological enemies, women. Given her childhood history, Elaine's fear and distrust of her own gender is understandable. Her positive experiences of women such as Mrs Finestein and Miss Stuart are not enough to prevent her from victimising a series of women in this novel as she unconsciously projects the abuse to which she has been subjected towards women in general.

Elaine is unable ever to rid herself of the sense that she is an 'outsider' in a group of women, and can never escape her feelings of hostility towards them. Elaine's two attacks on feminism, firstly in an interview (pp. 88–91), and subsequently following her move to Vancouver (pp. 378–9), resonate with resistance and apparently irrational fear. Women terrify Elaine as she knows they terrify men (p. 379), and her fear of them motivates all her actions against them. It is, however, significant that Elaine's icon of rescue is female: in the 'Lady of Perpetual Help', Elaine finds an image of matriarchal womanhood that ensures her survival.

In *Cat's Eye*, Margaret Atwood's examination of gender and society is less a feminist statement than a series of socio-cultural observations. Since these observations connect directly with, and comment upon, each of the central relationships in this novel, issues of gender must be identified as dominant themes in a narrative where a woman's survival following a terrifying ordeal at the hands of little girls is the key issue at stake.

NARRATIVE TECHNIQUES

Cat's Eye is a 'memory text', a novel where the notion of 'retrospection' conditions both the nature of the story told, and the techniques used to tell it. Concerned as it is with connecting the past with the present, the novel presents a stream of incidents from Elaine's Risley's life. This 'retrospective' is narrated from a present-tense position as the adult

Elaine abreacts event and offers comment upon it. As such, *Cat's Eye*
works through a double narrative where 'retrospective' and 'present-tense'
narratives are intersected.

While Elaine's 'present-tense' narrative is delivered from the
perspective of full knowledge of her memory-gap (these memories have
returned some years prior to her return to Toronto), the 'retrospective'
narrative, the bulk of the text, is delivered from a position of ignorance.
This narrative is marked by Elaine's inability to understand her responses,
emotions and reactions, while the 'present-tense' narrative reappraises the
meaning of all that has occurred. As a result, the two time-frames move
at different paces. The 'retrospective' narrative covers a span of over thirty
years and moves with speed. The 'present-tense' Toronto narrative, on
the other hand, covers a span of only a few days and offers a slackening
of pace. Beginning every new section, this narrative allows for a 'pause'
where the events and incidents of her life-story can be contemplated
before the 'retrospective' narrative is rejoined.

The notions of 'outer space' and 'inner space' are intersected in this
novel where observations of the physical geography of Toronto cause the
narrator to consider the events of her past. While the 'outer space'
observation contains strong elements of social documentary (for example,
in the record of a city desperately trying to prove its 'world class status'),
the 'inner space' explorations are introspective and trace a personal
history. The two commentaries are conjoined so that each flows
seamlessly into the other.

Scientific theory frequently intersects with narrative technique in
this novel. Stephen Hawking's question, 'Why do we remember the past,
and not the future?' (see Prefatory Material), connects with the narrator's
frequent references to events that have not yet occurred in her story.
These references provide 'echoes' of the 'future' and demonstrate
Stephen's point that 'Time is not a line but a dimension' (p. 3) where the
tenses coexist. In addition, Elaine's 'retrospective' narrative speeds up and
slows down according to the significance of the period recounted, and
this illustrates Stephen's argument that time 'runs faster in some places
than in others' (p. 219). Stephen's theoretical **discourse** is thus connected
with narrative strategy in *Cat's Eye*.

The narrative techniques discussed to this point belong to the
discursive narrative, that is, to Elaine's narrated account of her

experiences. However, a second narrative level is contained in this novel, this relating to the workings of Elaine's unconscious mind. The several paintings which the narrator describes, together with the dreams and 'visions' that she recalls, construct a **figural** narrative that is produced by the unconscious workings of Elaine's traumatised mind.

The figural narrative offers an alternative 'vision' of events to that offered by the discursive narrative. What neither Elaine nor the discursive narrative registers, the figural narrative illustrates: what her immediate perception conceals, her paintings, dreams and imagination reveal. As such, the figural narrative represents a 'sub-version' of the discursive narrative as Elaine's story is reconstructed in alternative and mutually completing forms. The figural narrative is therefore a visual autobiography, a coded version of the autobiography presented in the discursive narrative. Neither 'version' is complete without the other.

The complex techniques used by Atwood in this novel construct a narrative of several perspectives that produces versions and 'sub-versions' of the same story. The interaction between the figural and discursive narrative levels results in a **fictive autobiography** where issues of memory, knowledge, perception and self-perception are centralised.

LANGUAGE & STYLE

LANGUAGE

Margaret Atwood's use of language in this novel involves a range of devices and strategies. To begin with, *Cat's Eye* is a novel of several 'languages' and 'codes', all of which need to be 'deciphered' by the reader (and often by the narrator). Examples of the 'languages' that are featured within the text include 'pig Latin' (p. 168), and 'morse of feet' (p. 46), but the dominant non-verbal 'languages' in the novel are art and mathematics. Both are forms of communication that do not rely upon the spoken word; they are, to some extent, 'codes' using **symbols** to express a range of theoretical ideas or **allegorical** connections. The reader, like the narrator, must decipher these codes, and intersect them, to produce a 'version' of Elaine's life-story that is accurate and complete.

It is significant that both Elaine and Stephen select careers that involve non-verbal 'languages' since neither character is entirely comfortable within the world of words. Elaine is an introspective protagonist whose 'muteness' seems to characterise her for much of the text. Silent and withdrawn as a terrified child, 'watchful' as an adolescent, Elaine remains resistant to verbal communication in adult life. References to silence litter the text as a result. The fact that Elaine is skilled in reading boys' silences is emphasised (p. 237), while her marriage to Jon is conducted in a non-verbal 'language' involving hostile silences that create an atmosphere 'heavy with the unspoken' (p. 370). Silence therefore becomes yet another 'code' in this novel, and it frequently proves more expressive than verbal communication itself.

Elaine's unease in verbal territory is further indicated in the several verbal muddles with which she is associated throughout the text. Her painting *Falling Women*, for example (p. 268), is based upon a confusion over the term 'fallen women' (a Victorian term for prostitutes). Such errors are deliberate: Margaret Atwood has no wish to be confused with her protagonist, so she creates 'distance' between herself and her narrator by drawing this fundamental distinction between them.

Elaine's mistakes with words can produce intensely expressive images ('sopping' is surely more suggestive of tears than the correct 'sobbing', p. 172). This contributes to an overall poetic sensibility in the prose where the adult voice of the narrator joins the childish voice of her younger self to produce a series of startling descriptions and images. An example of the 'poetic prose' that results can be seen in the line, 'I am eating lost flight' (p. 131), which is a literal 'translation' of Professor Risley's anatomical lesson. Often, it is the brevity of such lines that lends impact.

A further aspect of the prose that both characterises Elaine and suggests poetic (and psychoanalytic) impulses is Elaine's connection between her senses and her memory. Repeatedly, scenes from her childhood are accessed through remembered smells, textures or colours: Professor Risley's laboratories, for example, are recalled through their 'mouse-dropping and formaldehyde smell' (p. 116). These precise sensory details also contribute to a sense of 'poetic prose' where colour, sound, texture and touch are registered as being central to memory and experience, as well as to the painting of 'word-pictures' (the project of the novelist).

While the novel revolves around Elaine's 'inner space' narrative, *Cat's Eye* remains centrally concerned with the 'outer space' territory of documentary realism. As a result, 'signs' from the 'real world' are recorded throughout the text: Atwood states that one reason for the inclusion of this detail was that she 'wanted a literary home for all those vanished *things* from my own childhood ... Part of fiction writing I think is a celebration of the physical world we know' (*Conversations*, pp. 236–7). Elaine's alertness to commercial slogans and puns causes the narrative to become littered with references to brand names, consumer items, and advertisement jingles. In addition, her awareness of changing times is registered in the frequent slang-terms, fashionable expressions, and popular songs quoted or recalled.

One future characteristic of Atwood's use of language in *Cat's Eye* deserves emphasis. The traumatic story recounted in this novel can cause the reader to overlook the wit and humour of Elaine's narrative. In fact, this is a consistently humorous text, and comedic devices abound. Elaine's tone of voice is a blend of wryness and pain, while an **ironic** note (especially in relation to herself) is consistently held by her. In addition, her recollection of her father in particular leads to moments of comic ventriloquism when his words are unexpectedly parroted by the young Elaine. For example, Professor Risley's views on religion are recorded without the aid of quotation marks, and this causes his words to merge imperceptibly with the voice of Elaine's childhood self: 'My father says he doesn't believe in brainwashing children. When you're grown up, then you can make up your own mind about religion, which has been responsible for a lot of wars and massacres in his opinion, as well as bigotry and intolerance' (p. 96). Similarly, Elaine ventriloquises Miss Lumley's rabid Imperialist dogma in a manoeuvre which draws attention to its ludicrousness (p. 79).

In a novel where several non-verbal 'languages' are employed and where a range of 'codes' must be deciphered (as in the painted **allegories** of personal trauma), Atwood utilises colloquialisms, poetic impulses, **metaphors** and ventriloquism in a web of connected styles and techniques. As a result, it is not simply Elaine's story that grips the reader: it is the language used by the novelist in its telling.

METAPHORS & IMAGERY

In *Cat's Eye*, 'blocks' of images and **metaphors** are constructed to create a network of meanings and associations throughout the narrative. These networks are developed through both the **discursive** and **figural** narratives, with several metaphorical networks and groups of images gathered together in the latter. Indeed, one of the reasons why Elaine's paintings prove a particularly rich source of analysis is that they provide a record of the dominant metaphorical networks forged in the novel.

These networks primarily involve an emphasis upon eyes and vision (Elaine is, after all, a painter), the heart, twinship and doubleness, mirrors, the notion of metamorphosis, and images of nothingness or void. Other networks of image and metaphor reinforce these dominant emphases: the concern with light and dark, for example, reinforces the metaphors circulating around vision, shape-shifting, and hauntings; similarly, the image (and metaphor) of the 'black hole' reinforces the image of void.

The most dominant metaphor in the novel is, of course, the cat's eye marble of the novel's title. To expand the meanings carried by the marble, and to link with Elaine's status as a painter, images relating to eyes and modes of vision echo through the novel (see Vision above). As a metaphor, the cat's eye marble represents a way of seeing without pain: it is a protective device whereby the young Elaine learns to 'see' as if through the cold glass of the cat's eye lens. To the traumatised child, the marble therefore becomes a type of talisman which she keeps hidden in her pocket to protect her from harm: 'With the help of its power', she recalls, 'I retreat back into my eyes' (p. 155). The properties of the marble thus become magical in their 'power', as when, years later, it operates as a reverse crystal-ball revealing to Elaine her 'life entire' (p. 398).

The metaphor of the heart connects with that of the cat's eye marble, and it also achieves a central significance in this novel. The connection between the two metaphors is clearly indicated in the painting *Unified Field Theory*, where the Virgin Mary holds an outsized cat's eye marble at the level of her heart (p. 408). Previously, the link between the heart and the eye has been registered in the idea that Mrs Smeath's 'bad heart floats in her body like an eye, an evil eye' (p. 180).

The metaphors of the heart and the eye thus become 'twinned' in a novel where an emphasis upon twinship and doubleness becomes a key metaphor. This emphasis is announced in the first **epigraph** to the novel taken from Eduardo Hughes Galeano's *Memory of Fire* where twinship becomes a key **motif** (see Prefatory Material). Following this epigraph, it comes as no surprise when pairs of twins begin to multiply as *Cat's Eye* develops. Stephen talks of twins in his discussion of time-travel (p. 219); Elaine is deeply disturbed by seeing a pair of dead human twins preserved in formaldehyde at the Conversat (p. 169), an event which curiously echoes her previous dream in which her mother had (in Elaine's imagination) miscarried twins (p. 166). In addition, the exchange of power between Cordelia and Elaine is effected through Elaine's assertion that she is one of a pair of twins, she being the vampire, the other being the 'daytime' version. This focus upon twinship, which recurs throughout the discursive narrative, draws the reader's attention to the way in which Cordelia and Elaine are twinned throughout.

This twinship, or 'doubleness', carries sinister connotations which have been discussed above (see Gothic). Images of mirrors reinforce these connotations since they provide a reflected self seen, effectively, in reverse: they 'double' the image of the onlooker to provide an identical 'twin'. This transaction implies supernatural activity when mirrors become associated with routes into another 'dimension' (see, for example, the story of the sisters on p. 211). The emphasis upon witches and ghosts throughout the novel sustains this emphasis upon a realm that is unseen but co-existent with the 'daytime' world of our perceptions. Meanwhile, the various lenses introduced throughout the text in turn reinforce the chain of images triggered by mirrors by providing routes into another unseen 'dimension', this one grounded in the physical world (biological cell-formations with microscopes, the cosmos with telescopes).

The several images of light and dark which recur throughout *Cat's Eye* connect metaphysical with physical regions in the same way as mirrors and lenses. Images of light gather around the themes of religion and science: in both **discourses**, 'light' is seen in terms of the 'light of knowledge' ('enlightenment' refers both to religious conversion and to a period of scientific advance). Further, 'light' is a religious metaphor since God's 'light' is perceived to spread love and moral value. Elaine's early exposure to religion inculcates her with an awareness of 'light' as a metaphor, while Stephen's discourses upon the speed of light, and upon the composition and behaviour of stars and the universe, lead her to decide that 'everything is made of solid light' (p. 220). The emphasis upon various manifestations of light clearly connects with the central cat's eye metaphor and with images of vision and 'sight' in general. Elaine's continuing attraction to forms of light is sustained into her adulthood; as a painter, for example, she is drawn to reflective surfaces and to 'objects that breathe out light; a luminous flatness' (p. 326). At the same time, she is terrified of its absence, and images of a menacing darkness pursue her: she refers to the 'black door' (p. 116) which leads onto her memories, and she defines her adult depressions in terms of a 'black vacancy' (p. 380). This clearly has its origins in her experience of 'live burial' where she recalls only 'a black square filled with nothing' (p. 107). Further, since the live burial is centrally implicated in the complex of emotions that have caused her to repress her memories, her physical burial in the ground becomes linked with her later 'buried' memories. Similarly, the 'black square' of the 'grave' is associated with the 'black holes' of the universe.

The metaphor of darkness is connected in *Cat's Eye* with images of nothingness or void. The word 'nothing' appears both in the crucial opening chapter ('Nothing goes away', p. 3) and in the equally crucial closing words of Elaine's story ('shining out of the midst of nothing', p. 421). The repetition of the word 'nothing' throughout the discursive narrative draws the reader's attention to its significance in relation to Elaine's psychic chaos where the 'black holes' of the cosmos are linked with Elaine's crushing personal sense of worthlessness and void. At several points in the novel, she feels that she is descending into a state of 'nothingness' where a sense of physical absence is compounded by a sense of psychological and emotional void. All this results from a childhood scarred by her experiences at the hands of Cordelia who had 'made me believe I was nothing' (p. 199).

In addition, images and metaphors circulating around the idea of metamorphosis and transformation echo throughout *Cat's Eye*. Initially, they emanate from Elaine's father's entomological interest in caterpillars (the insects most connected with physical metamorphosis), but as the allusions to shape-shifting gather, they are transformed into metaphors extending into psychological and supernatural territory (see Gothic). As

Elaine searches for new identities and disguises through cosmetics or clothing, she seeks constantly to metamorphose into someone else. In exactly the same way, Cordelia adopts multiple identities and 'faces' with such skill and regularity that her decision to become an actress is all but inevitable (see Characters). With only 'half a face' (p. 227), Cordelia's identity is permanently shifting as the Gothic theme of transformation finds an unmistakable echo here.

In *Cat's Eye*, networks of metaphors and images connect with, reinforce and expand each other so that no single cluster of meanings exists in isolation to others. In such a novel, **symbols** and motifs multiply, and those circulating around vertigo, the bridge, the ravine, dimensions, cellars and deadly nightshade also reward analysis.

CHARACTERISATION

ELAINE RISLEY

Elaine Risley, a middle-aged and well-known painter, is the central protagonist in this **fictive autobiography**. When we first encounter her, she is an isolated figure, wandering the Toronto streets of her childhood. As the narrative develops, a story of childhood torment is related in a stream of memories which have remained repressed for most of her adult life: they have returned only in Elaine's recent adulthood, immediately prior to her mother's death (see p. 398). We meet Elaine upon her first visit to Toronto following the return of her repressed memories.

The reader never manages to develop a clear idea of what Elaine looks like, and this is a deliberate strategy on Margaret Atwood's part. Through occasional glimpses during the narrative, we may construct *Half a Face* for Elaine (as she paints for Cordelia on p. 227), but this 'face' changes image so frequently in the novel that it is never either final or reliable. This physical instability is earnestly desired by Elaine who embarks upon a series of transformations throughout the narrative. Her constant need to reinvent herself is connected with her sense of insufficiency (of being judged and found wanting) that Cordelia, Grace and Carol had projected onto her as a child. As a result of this complex relationship with her appearance, it proves significant that the only image of herself that Elaine finds satisfying is one that has been distorted and disguised by a graffitied moustache (p. 20).

As the story of Elaine's childhood is traced, the development of her personality is explained. Her earliest childhood, though happy, was lonely, and her isolated early existence may have encouraged her predisposition towards introspection. It also planted in her a sense of 'otherness', particularly in relation to girls, and this is indicated in her alignment with the various 'displaced persons' whom she encounters. Elaine's enormous difficulty in expressing herself verbally is perhaps a manifestation of her sense of 'otherness'; it is also, of course, a result of her childhood torment when any words that she spoke would incur criticism, judgement and punishment at the hands of Cordelia, Grace and Carol. A habit of silence and repression was therefore established in her at an early age. This is one of the reasons why Elaine selects painting as a vocation: it enables her to 'articulate' without the aid of words.

One of Elaine's most striking characteristics is her refusal to 'feel' intense emotion except in retrospect. When, as a child, she reconstructs herself as someone who is 'happy as a clam: hard-shelled, firmly closed' (p. 201), she lays the foundations of a permanent resistance to painful experience. Closing herself off to the needs of others, she develops a 'mean mouth' (p. 234), rejects Cordelia twice (pp. 258–9, p. 359), coldly spurns Josef (p. 322), deserts Jon (p. 376), and delays grieving for the murdered Stephen (p. 392). Skilled at detaching herself from her own emotions, Elaine is also adept at detaching herself from those of others, remaining 'firmly closed' to their needs in case sharp pain should follow. The reader recognises that these are survival strategies and that the 'hard shell' does not characterise her: Elaine remains conscious of the suffering of anonymous strangers, is aware of the tragedies that blight the world, and is keenly vulnerable to others' sense of failure. In addition, as her paintings of Mrs Smeath reveal, she is capable of 'compassion'. Her thirst for vengeance is a hangover from the days when pain was inflicted upon her, but her capacity to forgive (as with Jon, p. 385, and as with Cordelia, p. 419) suggests that her essential humanity is never in question.

Despite Elaine's compassion for humanity in general, her hostility towards women is evident throughout the narrative. Given the traumas inflicted on Elaine by females as a child, this inter-gender hostility is not so irrational as it may seem, though it does cause her to respond aggressively at certain points in the narrative (pp. 90–91. p. 379). In addition, her quest for emotional inviolability leads her to play a range of power-games with men as well as women. Elaine has learned the importance of 'power' at an early age in her dealings with Cordelia, and her subsequent sense of being vulnerable to attack by an unseen persecutor leads her to pursue power unconsciously and to fear its loss.

Despite Elaine's characteristic introspection, and despite also her less sympathetic qualities, hers is a humorous and **ironic** voice. The reader responds positively to her self-deprecating remarks, to her witty consideration of puns and phrases, and to her comic appraisals of those around her. The reader finds it easy to sympathise with such a humorous and flawed narrator, particularly as her honesty in detailing her story often involves ruthless self-criticism.

If the reader experiences occasional difficulties in understanding Elaine's responses and motivations, then so too does Elaine herself. This is partly because the painful experiences that proved formative have been erased from her mind for much of her adult life. However, Elaine is also unable to know herself fully because she feels as though she is half 'missing': her 'other half', Cordelia, is absent. Elaine is, then, as alienated and isolated at the end of the novel as she is at the beginning. Her story has been an attempt to understand her past, but this attempt can only be partial while Cordelia remains an absent, silent enigma.

Swamped by images related to 'vision' from the beginning of her story to its conclusion, Elaine, through her painter's 'eye', strives to connect 'sight' with 'insight' as she reconstructs her history. **Paradoxically,** perhaps, Elaine 'sees' the physical properties of her world with astonishing clarity (as a painter, she 'sees' colour and texture particularly clearly), whilst remaining 'blind' to the essentials of her experience. Throughout the 'present-tense' narrative, and in our final view of her, this experience consists of a chain of negatives: absence, silence and void. A sense of loss characterises the final chapter of the novel, and it is this which potentially conditions our ultimate response towards Atwood's alienated, fractured protagonist.

ELAINE'S PARENTS

Elaine's parents are highly unconventional in the world of 1950s suburban Toronto. Her father is a research scientist (an entomologist) and is liberal in his outlook. He is a humanist like his daughter, and a rationalist for whom religion is responsible for only 'bigotry and intolerance' (p. 96). His ideas and opinions are ventriloquised by the young Elaine throughout the novel, and his apparently eccentric predictions concerning the environment gradually take on the form of accurate prophecy. His voice is the conduit for the novelist's own ecological concerns.

Elaine provides a short but detailed summary of her father's life-story half way through the narrative when we are told that his background was one of grinding poverty (p. 217). His ambition had been to train as a pilot during the Second World War but he was prevented from doing so because his scientific work was considered vital to the war effort. In the course of the narrative, Professor Risley suffers further disappointments: his wife miscarries their third child, Elaine rejects botany in favour of art, and, in his greatest tragedy, his brilliant son is murdered in a senseless act of contingent violence. He emerges from these painful experiences as a man of considerable character and as a kindly and eccentric presence. However, though his benign aspect contrasts him with most of the other terrifying fathers that Elaine encounters in her childhood, he nevertheless remains a peripheral presence in the novel.

Mrs Risley is as unconventional as her husband and, having little interest in domesticity, seems more than content in the years of their nomadic wilderness existence. When finally resident in Toronto, she adopts the standard dress conventions of her society, but remains triumphantly unconcerned with her physical appearance and with her neighbours' opinion of her. Despite her likeable eccentricity, however, a shadow intrudes in Mrs Risley's relationship with her daughter when she proves powerless to rescue her daughter from Cordelia, Grace and Carol. Elaine unconsciously holds this against her mother all her adult life (as is acknowledged on p. 397). In turn, Mrs Risley obviously suffers a sense of guilt about her handling of Elaine's 'bad time' (pp. 394–5).

When the Risleys leave Toronto and move permanently to the wilderness spaces of Northern Canada, it is as though they vacate Elaine's life for ever. However, Elaine's conflicting and confused attitudes towards her mother are expressed in the painting *Pressure Cooker* (pp. 150–1), a series of images that attempt to render her 'timeless'.

STEPHEN

Stephen shows marked signs of eccentricity from a young age, and his academic brilliance in the fields of mathematics and astrophysics ultimately develops into genius. He and Elaine are close as children and engage in war-games and coded exchanges. Stephen has a passionate interest in collecting items (whether marbles or 'stars') and his fanatical pursuit of a new hobby (comics, chemistry or astronomy) absorbs him totally. To Elaine as a teenager, he begins to seem like an odd stranger, and his parents also begin to feel alienated from their increasingly manic, genius son.

Stephen effectively exits the narrative when he leaves home to attend university. He reappears only once when he delivers a scientific paper at Toronto University (Chapter 59). His occasional postcards to Elaine inform her of recent developments in his life (including marriage and divorce), and give the impression that he does not fully belong to the physical dimension of 'real' people (birthdays, for example, have no 'meaning' for him, p. 334). His senseless murder seems a tragic but appropriate death given his incompatibility with the human world. It is as if his level of genius prevents him from either understanding or developing human engagement: his distrust of, and resistance to, any 'language' other than mathematics could be seen as evidence of his unease in the human 'dimension'. In a theoretical, 'universal' realm of his own, his scientific discourses in the education of Elaine provide a framework for her paintings. In converting the abstract into the **figural** through her art, Elaine conjoins the universal with the human principle in a way that Stephen never manages to do. Stephen features in the painting *Picoseconds*, described on pp. 405–6.

CORDELIA

Cordelia, Elaine's childhood tormentor, provides the other 'half' of Elaine's 'face' (p. 227). Cordelia is a 'missing person' for most of the novel, yet her constant background presence, lurking on the periphery of Elaine's vision (as in her nightmare of p. 250) means that she is as central to the narrative as is Elaine. Since the two are 'twins', this is not surprising. Cordelia is Elaine's 'dark double', or her mirrored reflection: she haunts both Elaine's conscious and unconscious mind just as she haunts the entire narrative.

Cordelia's association with the supernatural and with dark, demonic forces is sustained throughout. One of her informing characteristics is her witchlike capacity for shape-shifting and metamorphosis: as in the case of Elaine, the reader never manages to construct a reliable physical impression of Cordelia because the transformations through which she passes are so radical as to produce several contesting 'versions' of her. A description is supplied of Cordelia as a child on p. 70, but the specific detail rendered here is later undermined as her image alters beyond recognition. She becomes a flashy teenager (p. 204), a bloated mess (p. 258), a sophisticated, gaunt artiste (p. 300), and a damaged, transfigured mental patient (p. 356). However, her most constant image is of an 'airy spirit' in *The Tempest* where her insubstantiality suggests that she is both 'absent' and 'present' at the same time.

As Stephen so perceptively comments of her, 'Cordelia has a tendency to exist' (p. 242). This proves to be Cordelia's defining moment. Appearing most regularly as a disembodied voice and image in Elaine's mind, Cordelia 'exists' largely in other people's memories and in other people's 'eyes'. This is what Elaine is referring to when she notes on p. 411 that the 'part of herself I could give back' to Cordelia is her 'reflection'.

Just as Elaine's damaged psyche is a result of her childhood experiences, so too is Cordelia a result of her formative experiences. However, where Elaine has suffered at the hands of agencies external to her family (in the form of the girls), Cordelia has suffered within the family unit. Her family is 'gifted' (p. 72) and she is surrounded by the beautiful, accomplished role-models of her mother and sisters. Cordelia is clearly aware of the fact that she is not 'gifted' in the same way as them (see p. 72). The family of women is presided over by a charming but imposing father-figure whom Cordelia is unable to please (in an echo of Lear's youngest daughter in Shakespeare's *King Lear*). One critic has even suggested that Cordelia may be the victim of incestuous child-abuse at his hands, though there is no direct textual evidence to support this theory (see Sharon Rose Wilson, 1993).

Cordelia is subject to a continuous stream of correction and criticism from all her family members. It is this atmosphere of disapproval that she projects onto the vulnerable Elaine, and she ventriloquises the words of admonishment that are used against her. Cordelia's victimisation of Elaine is an attempt to exorcise the feelings of inadequacy from which she herself suffers. In transferring this sense of inadequacy onto Elaine, she hopes to reduce the pain that she feels in relation to it. This is what Elaine realises on her final visit to the ravine (p. 419).

Cordelia's talent for ventriloquism and mimicry, together with her early interest in play-acting and performance, lead her towards a career as an actress. Her onstage roles allow her to 'become' another person in the ultimate transformation. However, Cordelia, having no firm identity of her own, and being accustomed to 'trying on' new identities in an effort to find one that pleases her father, confuses the boundary between performance and 'real life' so that her existence becomes a continual 'performance'. This is made clear when she reappears in the text as a sophisticated actress and Elaine notes of her, 'She is like someone making herself up as she goes along. She's improvising' (p. 301). From this position, it is just a short step to Cordelia's fragile sense of self fragmenting completely, causing her to spin into breakdown. Her permanent physical absence following Elaine's second refusal to help her escape from psychological disintegration could equally be explained by either resentment of Elaine, a conclusive slide into mental disturbance, or by a successful suicide-bid.

All Cordelia's childhood actions can be retrospectively seen by Elaine (and by the reader) as a 'cry for help'. Her shoplifting, for example, provided her with 'something I could have', as she explains to Elaine when they meet again after the absence of years (p. 303); similarly, the holes she had dug in the ground were an attempt to build 'some place that was all mine, where nobody could bug me' (p. 252). In her quest for outright 'possession' of items or spaces that belonged only to her, Cordelia was in pursuit of identity and sanctuary.

Finally, Cordelia remains for the reader (and for Elaine), the burned sister who inhabits the mirror and then her sister in the grim horror story (p. 211). However, when these ideas achieve figural expression in the painting *Half a Face* (p. 227), it becomes clear that the 'twinned' identities of Cordelia and Elaine cause confusion about which sister is 'possessing' the other, and about where the boundary between Cordelia and Elaine actually lies. Only when their two reflections are put together does one identity emerge. When Cordelia fails to reappear at the end of the novel, the acknowledgement of Cordelia's now permanent 'absence' characterises Elaine's final sense of loss.

OTHER CHARACTERS

CORDELIA'S PARENTS

Cordelia's family name is never supplied. Her father is a member of the terrifying group that Elaine as a child identifies as 'other girls' fathers'. Largely absent from his all-female household (since he is at work all day), Cordelia's father enjoys a position of absolute authority within his home. He is a large, handsome and charming man, and his wife, Perdie and Mirrie tease and humour him successfully. However, there is a dark side to Cordelia's father, indicated in particular by the way in which he is described as 'wolvish' (p. 249). He clearly dislikes Cordelia who withers under the glare of his 'disappointment' (p. 73). A menacing, powerful figure, Cordelia's father is central to any 'version' of the past that Elaine's 'twin' could supply.

In contrast to her imposing husband, Cordelia's mother is 'tiny, fragile, absent-minded' (p. 73). 'Gifted' and artistic like her accomplished daughters, she is a woman of style and taste who decorates her home with sophistication. Her relationship with Cordelia is not analysed in the course of the narrative, though it is likely that her attitudes towards her youngest daughter reflect those of her husband.

PERDIE & MIRRIE

Cordelia's two beautiful older sisters are named after Shakespeare's Perdita (from *The Winter's Tale*) and Miranda (from *The Tempest*): as such, they are both aligned with romantic heroines while Cordelia is named after the doomed tragic heroine who is largely absent from Shakespeare's *King Lear*.

Unlike Cordelia, Perdie and Mirrie are said to be 'gifted' (Perdie in ballet, Mirrie in music), and their appearances fulfil all the requisites of conventional 'femininity'. Their manner towards Cordelia and her friends is deeply patronising and their mode of speech is snobbish and comically pretentious. They sustain the atmosphere of disapproval and criticism which swamps Cordelia within her family, repeating and enforcing their father's negative assessment of her.

GRACE SMEATH

Grace is a year older than Elaine and Carol, and is the 'favoured' friend whose attention and company is sought and competed for by the others. It is Grace who initiates Elaine into the world of household catalogues and film-star magazines, and who indirectly introduces Elaine to religion. She is also centrally implicated in the traumas inflicted upon Elaine, though she is not the ringleader as Mrs Risley believes. Cordelia is responsible for devising the various torments inflicted upon Elaine, but Grace is guilty of implementing them. She is in charge of Sunday surveillance and seems to have justified her unkindness by accepting her mother's belief in the 'justice' of punishing a 'heathen'.

Grace disappears from the novel following the ravine incident, though two further references are made to her: Cordelia cruelly mocks her (pp. 230–1), and Elaine at first believes that Grace is the ink-throwing religious fanatic who defaces her painting (pp. 352–3). However, Grace is effectively displaced in Elaine's traumatised psyche by images of her forbidding mother.

MRS SMEATH & MR SMEATH

Mrs Smeath is inseparable from the traumas of Elaine's childhood, and is associated most obviously with mean-minded malice, and with the inhumanity of fanatical religious judgement. Her 'bad heart' represents not only a medical condition, but also suggests her lack of compassion and kindness. The description of Mrs Smeath (pp. 57–8) involves a chain of revolting physical characteristics that reveal the level of apparently irrational hatred that Elaine feels towards her even into adulthood. This hatred (deriving from the overheard conversation, pp. 179–80) is clearly expressed in the numerous images she later paints of her persecutor. When she views these paintings, Elaine recognises the 'malice' of her images, but it is only at the end of the narrative that she can also recognise the fact that Mrs Smeath had been a 'displaced person' as she herself was, and that she has unconsciously painted a sense of 'defeat' and 'melancholy' into her 'unloved' eyes (p. 405). Elaine thus refuses the philosophy of vengeance with which Mrs Smeath is associated ('An eye for an eye', p. 405), and can even wish that she had imbued the various images of her with more 'mercy' (p. 405). Nevertheless, Mrs Smeath remains connected with harsh, smug homilies such as '*It serves her right*' (p. 321), and it is her voice that Elaine hears whenever she is prone to feelings of self-disgust, guilt or confusion.

Mr Smeath, on the other hand, is a benign presence in the narrative. He is exonerated from the malice and religious fanaticism of his wife, and seems as 'alien' to the Smeath household and mentality as does Elaine herself. His is the one voice of light relief at Smeath Sunday lunches, and he particularly favours making vulgar comments at the dinner table. Elaine feels the kindness of this short, flabby man to be evidence of her close affiliation with males in contrast to her ambivalent relationship with females. Mr Smeath, she feels, is owed her loyalty because he is her fellow 'conspirator'; he is 'subversive' of the self-righteousness and judgement represented by his wife and, through her, by women in general (p. 126).

CAROL CAMPBELL

Carol is Elaine's first friend at school, but she later becomes the least important member of the group of four girls. She is an unlikeable child, given to crying noisily when picked upon by Cordelia, and weak in her complicity with Cordelia's victimisation of Elaine. She is also contemptuous of Elaine's ramshackle home, prone to informing on her friends, and constantly currying favour at school. Later, she will flirt determinedly with boys.

Carol is as much a product of her environment as the other girls in the group, and her behaviour is largely a result of responses learned within the family unit. Her family is highly conformist (as her mother's fondness for chintz fabrics, cold perms, and twin-sets reveals), and her father is one of the shadowy figures of male authority who enter the domestic sphere at nightfall to maintain discipline. Beaten with a belt by him when she transgresses, Carol is a victim of physical abuse just as Cordelia is a victim of psychological and emotional abuse.

MISS LUMLEY

One of Elaine's first teachers at school, Miss Lumley is a terrifying presence. A fanatical Imperialist, her view of countries not ruled by Britain is filled with images of uncivilised heathens, and she teaches the children to hero-worship the British Royal Family. Her idiotic ideology is a sign of the contempt the adult narrator feels for this bully. Her menacing presence is, however, comically undermined by the rumour that she habitually wears huge pairs of navy-blue bloomers. These hideous items of clothing lead to Elaine's crushing realisation as a child that the 'shameful' secrets they hide are shared by her, since they are both female (p. 81). Miss Lumley and her bloomers are therefore central to Elaine's fear of, and hostility towards, her own gender.

MISS STUART

In contrast to Miss Lumley, Miss Stuart is a thoroughly benign figure. She is a sympathetic teacher with a keen interest in art, and she stimulates the children's imaginations with exotic ideas of other nations which are, in contrast to Miss Lumley's 'versions' of 'crafty' natives, filled with cheerfulness, colour and freedom (p. 161).

Miss Stuart is Scottish and, as a 'displaced person', recognises Elaine's sense of 'displacement' and alienation. When she looks at the blacked-out picture that Elaine accidentally produces, her 'I see' in response suggests that she genuinely understands the nature of Elaine's distress (p. 162). A secret drinker who smothers tea-time whiskey fumes with a nurse's mask, Miss Stuart's kindness towards the young Elaine is acknowledged in the painting *Three Muses* (pp. 406–7).

VICTOR BANERJI

Victor Banerji is a research student from India who is supervised in his studies by Elaine's father; he later becomes a junior colleague of his at the University of Toronto. The young Elaine feels a special affinity with him because she senses that he is another 'displaced person' like herself: she 'sniffs out' his misery, and notes his bitten fingernails and his 'dark appalled eyes' (p. 129). She likes to see him regularly to ensure that he is surviving because she feels that if he is managing to do so, then so can she (p. 158). A victim of racial prejudice, Victor Banerji is eventually forced to return to India because it is implied that he is unable to win promotion in Canada. His final appearance in the novel is in the painting *Three Muses* (pp. 406–7).

MRS FINESTEIN

Mrs Finestein is Jewish and, as such, is yet another 'displaced person' with whom the young Elaine had felt a special connection: indeed, she dreams that Mr Banerji and Mrs Finestein are her real parents (p. 166). Mrs Finestein stands out from her neighbours on account of her exotic tastes, but this very 'otherness' triggers a stream of racist invective from Cordelia, Grace and Carol who repeat their parents' offensive comments about Jews. Mrs Finestein later applies the dreaded phrase 'letting yourself go' to Elaine in her beatnik phase, but the words are less judgemental than comically concerned, coming from her sympathetic lips (p. 277).

Mrs Finestein appears in the painting *Three Muses*, and Elaine notes that 'death-camp ashes' must have haunted her in the wake of the Second World War (p. 407). Together with Miss Stuart and Mr Banerji, two other 'displaced persons' who had shown her 'casual' but life-sustaining kindness as a child, Mrs Finestein is remembered with affection and gratitude by the adult Elaine (pp. 406–7).

JOSEF HRBIK

It is Hrbik who is most directly associated with the idea of 'displaced persons' in this novel since Elaine's life-drawing teacher is a refugee from the Hungarian Revolution: the male students use the phrase against him when they deride him (p. 281). Like Elaine, Hrbik is haunted by his memories which he attempts to repress but which penetrate his dreams.

In his mid-thirties and apparently attractive, Hrbik enjoys unprofessional relationships with his students, including Elaine who mistakenly feels that is he in need of 'rescue' from the clutches of Susie, another student (p. 286). However, following Susie's terrifying abortion,

OTHER CHARACTERS continued

Elaine feels that Hrbik has become a burden on her and she begins to find his demands stifling. Eventually, she abandons him (p. 322).

Later, Hrbik fulfils his dream of making films in the United States and produces a 'version' of the triangular relationship between himself, Elaine and Susie in a film that Elaine sees. This 'version' reveals that Hrbik had never been able to view women as 'real' and had been unable to understand that women's 'craziness' does not necessarily result from their relationships with men (p. 365). Elaine decides that Hrbik had belonged to 'the world of dreams', that they had used each other, and that her final cruelty towards him had been necessary to her survival (p. 365).

SUSIE

Initially, Elaine's characteristically negative feelings towards women cause her to misjudge Susie, a fellow-student in her life-drawing class. Misled by her blonde hair and heavy make-up, Elaine categorises her as a manipulating predator, and she observes Susie closely before moving in on her lover, Hrbik. However, following Susie's abortion, Elaine is forced to reassess her rival, and she realises that Susie was never anything more than 'a nice girl playing dress-ups' (p. 320). Though Susie is, for Elaine, an example of the disasters that can befall women, and though she gloats when she begins to 'let herself go' (pp. 318–9), Elaine nevertheless comes to respect Susie a great deal more than she does Hrbik.

JON

Elaine had been one of Jon's drinking partners when they were art students together. He seems to have talent as an artist, and his work shifts according to new trends: his 'potential', though, finally comes to nothing (p. 265), and he ends up working as a special-effects designer on horror films. As a student, he had voiced sexist attitudes towards women artists, and he consistently undermines Elaine's paintings (see p. 327). However, his appeal to Elaine is that together they can escape the world of 'mothers' (p. 318) by behaving as though they are irresponsible adolescents. When marriage and children remove this freedom from them, their marriage disintegrates.

Jon and Elaine eventually divorce, having been a 'shark to one another, but also lifeboat' (p. 17). Elaine does not blame Jon for the wreckage of their marriage since 'Whatever he did to me, I did back, and maybe worse' (p. 378). Jon is implicated in the idea of men as the 'jagged', perilous rocks that are 'without volition' (and thus without malevolence) in the painting *Falling Women* (p. 268). Finally, he and Elaine part from each other as 'survivors, of each other' (p. 17).

BEN
Ten years older than his wife, Ben clearly gives Elaine a sense of emotional security. He is a travel agent, and Elaine welcomes his straightforward simplicity after Jon's neurotic complexity (she describes him as an 'apple, after a prolonged and gluttonous binge', p. 381). Ben admires the skill with which Elaine draws hands, but he does not understand her art at all.

Although Elaine makes love to Jon when in Toronto, her deep affection for her second husband is obviously sincere. Elaine simply sees her lives in Toronto and Vancouver as separate: Ben belongs to her Vancouver existence where she is 'another person' living a different kind of life. His late entry into the novel, together with the fact that he never appears in the narrative 'in person', attests to the fact that it is the Toronto 'retrospective' which is the chief concern here.

PART FOUR

TEXTUAL ANALYSIS

The three passages selected for analysis in this section each involve the ravine – the locus of Elaine's trauma. The analyses demonstrate the way in which Elaine's life-story is represented in different 'versions', each of which are 'sub-versions' which expand the meanings of the others. In the first extract, Elaine's past-tense story is detailed in the present-tense **discursive** mode: here, the ravine belongs first to the physical world but gradually melts into unconscious territories. In the second extract, the memories and psychic connections associated with the ravine are represented in the painting *Unified Field Theory*: the painting is therefore a **figural** narrative of the ravine 'vision'. In the third extract, Elaine finally returns to the ravine in the present-tense discursive narrative having spent her visit to Toronto in a gradual approach towards it: here, conscious and unconscious responses to the area are at last integrated as Cordelia's 'ghost' is laid to rest and as the ravine is returned to the dimension of the physical world. The three extracts therefore provide representations of the ravine in two psychological registers (the conscious and the unconscious), and in two narrative modes (the figural and the discursive).

TEXT **1**   (PAGE 189)

I know I should get up and walk home, but it seems easier to stay here, in the snow, with the little pellets of ice caressing my face gently. Also I'm very sleepy. I close my eyes.

I hear someone talking to me. It's like a voice calling, only very soft, as if muffled. I'm not sure I've heard it at all. I open my eyes with an effort. The person who was standing on the bridge is moving through the railing, or melting into it. It's a woman, I can see the long skirt now, or is it a long cloak? She isn't falling, she's coming down towards me as if walking, but there's nothing for her to walk on. I don't have the energy to be frightened. I lie in the snow, watching her with lethargy, and with a sluggish curiosity. I would like to be able to walk on air like that.

Now she's quite close. I can see the white glimmer of her face, the dark scarf or hood around her head, or is it her hair? She holds out her arms to me and I feel a surge of happiness. Inside her half-open cloak there's a glimpse of red. It's her heart, I think. It must be her heart, on the outside of her body, glowing like neon, like a coal.

Then I can't see her any more. But I feel her around me, not like arms but like a small wind of warmer air. She's telling me something.

You can go home now, she says. *It will be all right. Go home.*

I don't hear the words out loud, but this is what she says.

In this passage, the young Elaine occupies a borderline position between sleep and waking, consciousness and unconsciousness, and life and death. The extremity of her situation has led to this threatening position. At this stage in the retrospective narrative, Elaine is at her most desperate and terrified, the ravine has assumed nightmare proportions in a projection of her inner chaos, and the weather conditions are unusually severe. This combination of circumstances produces an internal and external situation that forces a crisis. Elaine emerges from her near-death experience equipped with a power that she cannot rationalise, having seen a 'vision' that she cannot understand.

The power that Elaine acquires following this incident seems to derive from supernatural or unconscious levels that have produced her 'vision'. Though she will later accept that 'I know this didn't happen' (p. 418), she clearly recalls seeing some kind of image in this passage. It is likely that the 'vision' was, in fact, no more than a product of Elaine's fear, psychic tension, and hypothermic condition as she lapses into a semi-coma (she recalls that she was 'sleepy' and had closed her eyes). However, as the light fades and as darkness gathers, the ravine area metamorphoses from a physical location into a supernatural space capable of producing 'visions'.

This 'vision' is described in vague terms: Elaine cannot be sure whether 'it' wore a long skirt or a long cloak, and cannot determine whether a scarf, hood, or hair framed the 'white glimmer of her face'. The detail is generally nonspecific but conveys an overall impression, colour and shape. At the same time, certain details prove particularly memorable: Elaine recalls seeing a 'glimpse' of red in the folds of the 'half-open cloak' which she connects with the externalised heart of 'Our Lady of Perpetual Help' as represented in the cheap picture she had found on a pavement (p. 182). It also connects with the 'vision' that she had produced previously where the heart is aligned with Elaine's red purse (p. 184). It is clear, then, that the vague detail of the 'vision' accords with images previously lodged in Elaine's unconscious as produced by iconographic representations of the Virgin Mary in which she has placed her faith. To Elaine, this representation has come to connote rescue, pity and the possibility of survival, and while the physical properties of the image are nebulous, Elaine's emotional and psychological response to it is distinctly recalled.

Elaine describes feeling a 'surge of happiness' and a sense of protection as she likens the sensation emanated by the presence to 'a small wind of warmer air'. The silent 'voice' that Elaine hears is produced by her new faith in survival that the imagined 'vision' has produced. The issue of communication is foregrounded here in that it connects with the novel's constant exploration of modes of expression that are not verbally produced (mathematics, painting and so on). Communication is also a key issue in the way in which this incident is related: as Elaine relives (or abreacts) the scene, it is as if she is back in the ravine as a child. Statements such as 'I would like to be able to walk on air like that' are delivered in the voice of the nine-year-old, not the adult. The short sentences produce the sense that the narrator is supplying details as they occur. The questions ('or is it a long cloak?) do not invite response but convey the sense that Elaine is reliving the scene and trying to determine what she is seeing.

It is an **irony** of *Cat's Eye* that Elaine Risley repeatedly fails to see what is in front of her eyes (as in her inability to 'see' what her paintings mean), but is able to see what is *not* in front of her eyes in the form of 'visions'. There is, then, a world of difference in this novel between 'vision' and 'a vision', and it is only upon Elaine's final return to the ravine that the 'snow' in her eyes 'withdraws like smoke' (p. 419), enabling her to 'see clearly' for the first time.

TEXT 2   (PAGE 408)

The last painting is *Unified Field Theory*. It's a vertical oblong, larger than the other paintings. Cutting across it a little over a third up is a wooden bridge. To either side of the bridge are the tops of trees, bare of leaves, with a covering of snow on them, as after a heavy moist snowfall. This snow is also on the railing and struts of the bridge.

Positioned above the top railing of the bridge, but so her feet are not quite touching it, is a woman dressed in black, with a black hood or veil covering her hair. Here and there on the black of her dress or cloak there are pinpoints of light. The sky behind her is the sky after sunset; at the top of it is the lower half of the moon. Her face is partly in shadow.

She is the Virgin of Lost Things. Between her hands, at the level of her heart, she holds a glass object: an oversized cat's eye marble, with a blue centre.

Underneath the bridge is the night sky, as seen through a telescope. Star upon star, red, blue, yellow, and white, swirling nebulae, galaxy upon galaxy: the universe, in its incandescence and darkness. Or so you think. But there are also stones down there, beetles and small roots, because this is the underside of the ground.

At the lower edge of the painting the darkness pales and merges to a lighter tone, the clear blue of water, because the creek flows there, underneath the earth, underneath the bridge, down from the cemetery. The land of the dead people.

This passage provides an example of the way in which the **figural** narrative in this novel operates. Here, images associated with the ravine in Elaine's psyche are gathered together in a 'unified' representation of the dominant **metaphors** and images of Elaine's life story. Since Elaine encounters *Unified Field Theory* 'last', it seems that this is one of her most recent paintings (the exhibition has been arranged chronologically). As such, it differs from the majority of the paintings described in this novel since it is likely that it was composed following the return of Elaine's memory of her two-year trauma. The canvas can therefore be defined as a pictorial autobiography which has been painted in the full 'light' of the artist's self-knowledge.

All the paintings described in *Cat's Eye* provide a figural corollary to the **discursive** narrative. Where the latter uses words to describe

Elaine's childhood, the former uses painted images to tell the same story in **allegorical** terms. As a result, the painting described in this extract replicates the 'vision' in the ravine previously described in the first extract: the 'Virgin of Lost Things' hovers above the ground, is dressed in black though it is unclear whether a hood or a veil covers her hair (as before), and her face, previously a 'white glimmer' (p. 189) is now 'partly in shadow' (a similarly amorphous sense is created). In the 'unified' representation detailed here, however, these images have become less of a blend between the 'real' and the 'imagined' than an allegorical representation involving a complex of psychic associations and metaphors which removes it from the territory of the 'real'.

A variety of significant images and **motifs** from Elaine's childhood have been added to the image so that the painting becomes a repository for the charged emblems of her trauma. The oversized cat's eye marble (potentially suggesting a type of crystal ball, also implied on p. 398) is held at the level of the Virgin's heart. This externalised image of goodness has been contrasted with Mrs Smeath's internalised 'bad heart' throughout the narrative. Further, the sky underneath the bridge is seen as through the lens of a telescope, this inviting connections not only with Stephen's theoretical lecture (titled 'Unified Field Theory', p. 331), but also with astrology in general. In the early sections of the novel, stars were seen as objects of wonder before religious instruction persuaded Elaine to view them as the watchful eyes of a judgemental God. In addition, the representation of 'the underside of the ground' is a clear echo of Elaine's experience in the 'grave' (p. 108), the point at which she 'lost power' (p. 107). The result is a metaphorically registered record of pain and survival.

This being a novel, of course, the paintings are described to the reader using the medium of words. As such, the paintings are, literally, 'word-pictures': words lead the reader to 'see' the paintings, to imagine what they look like. The images described in the paintings are not 'explained' to the reader in direct terms, and it is left to the reader to attach the relevant meanings to them. This is made possible by the discursive narrative, so that what is produced is a life-story 'written' in two different versions. Together, they represent a 'unified' version of events, but only when Elaine (and the reader) is equipped with both the figural and the discursive 'angles of vision' can synthesis between them be achieved.

TEXT 3   (PAGES 418–9)

I know that if I turn, right now, and look ahead of me along the path, someone
will be standing there. At first I think it will be myself, in my old jacket, my blue
knitted hat. But then I see that it's Cordelia. She's standing halfway up the hill,
gazing back over her shoulder. She's wearing her grey snowsuit jacket but the hood
is back, her head is bare. She has the same green wool kneesocks, sloppily down
around her ankles, the brown school brogues scuffed at the toes, one lace broken
and knotted, the yellowish-brown hair with the bangs falling into her eyes, the
eyes grey-green.

It's cold, colder. I can hear the rustle of the sleet, the water moving under the ice.

I know she's looking at me, the lopsided mouth smiling a little, the face closed
and defiant. There is the same shame, the sick feeling in my body, the same
knowledge of my own wrongness, awkwardness, weakness; the same wish to be
loved; the same loneliness; the same fear. But these are not my own emotions any
more. They are Cordelia's; as they always were.

I am the older one now, I'm the stronger. If she stays here any longer she will
freeze to death; she will be left behind, in the wrong time. It's almost too late.

I reach out my arms to her, bend down, hands open to show I have no weapon. *It's
all right*, I say to her. *You can go home now.*

The snow in my eyes withdraws like smoke.

When I turn, finally, Cordelia is no longer there. Only a middle-aged woman,
pink-cheeked and bareheaded, coming down the hill towards me, in jeans and a
heavy white pullover, with a dog on a green leash, a terrier. She passes me smiling,
a civil, neutral smile.

There's nothing more for me to see. The bridge is only a bridge, the river a river,
the sky is a sky. This landscape is empty now, a place for Sunday runners. Or not
empty: filled with whatever it is by itself, when I'm not looking.

The painting *Unified Field Theory* suggests that the ravine area has
become overladen with traumatic connections in Elaine's mind, and she
has become so terrified of the site that she has been unable to return to it
until this point in the novel. Throughout the present-tense Toronto
narrative, Elaine approaches it in ever-decreasing circles, gathering

courage to confront it. In returning to the site of her gravest distress, Elaine knows that she must 'lay her ghosts to rest'. In effect, this involves cutting her ties with her **metaphorical** twin, Cordelia, breaking free of the hold she still retains over her, and thus relinquishing the past. Only then can she hesitantly move towards a livable future.

In this extract, the ravine again becomes a site of supernatural encounter as Elaine feels a 'presence' standing behind her. Initially, she thinks that this is a 'ghost' of her nine-year-old self, but then she 'sees' that it is the ghost of Cordelia as a child. That she 'sees' this 'ghost' is important because Elaine has not actually turned her head in response to the 'presence': she 'sees' in her mind's eye only (again successfully managing to 'see' what is *not* there). Nevertheless, she describes the image of the young Cordelia and, through repetition, pays particular attention to her eyes: 'the bangs falling into her eyes, the eyes grey-green' (p. 419). Immediately, she feels overwhelmed with self-disgust, but with new perception, she feels also that these emotions are being projected from the image of Cordelia, just as they always had been. As such, she had merely absorbed Cordelia's projected pain and her susceptibility to this exchange had led to her childhood trauma. Significantly, given the connection between 'sight' and 'insight' in this novel, Elaine's accurate insight into her relationship with Cordelia is registered in terms of clearing vision.

The tenuous 'power' that Elaine had enjoyed over Cordelia following her vampire story (p. 233) now becomes concrete as she assumes the position of command: 'I am the older one now, I'm the stronger' (p. 419). Perceiving Cordelia's imagined presence to be a 'ghost' caught in a time-warp, she likens her plight to that of herself as a child when she was caught in the ravine and on the verge of freezing to death. In addition, Cordelia is aligned with some kind of terrified creature, likely to turn upon its 'rescuer': when Elaine opens her hands to 'show I have no weapon', she is attempting to calm the frightened, desperate 'ghost' that she perceives. She then assumes the role of the 'vision' in 'rescuing' Cordelia from her plight, and echoes her words in laying Cordelia's image to rest. Instantly, she is released from the trance-like state that has produced these sensations.

When Elaine finally turns to inspect the space behind her in which she had perceived Cordelia's childhood presence, she sees only a middle-aged woman walking a dog, 'a terrier'. The specificity of this unnecessary detail returns us to the real world. The bridge and the ravine are finally reconverted into features belonging to the physical dimension. Their alignment with a borderline territory between the conscious and the unconscious evaporates: 'The bridge is only a bridge, the river a river, the sky is a sky'. This flat statement, stripped of metaphorical associations, positions the area as a prosaic location rather than as a carrier of unconscious meaning. With fresh 'sight' and 'insight', Elaine has neutralised the menacing connotations of the ravine, and she can finally accept that the area exists when she is not there to see it. As such, she accepts that it exists independently of her unconscious.

In facing the ravine area, Elaine has effectively stared down her 'ghosts'. She has confronted her memories and has stripped them of terror, and she can now move forward, across a metaphorical bridge of time, to confront her future.

The ravine has, in each of the three extracts, proved capable of radical metamorphosis. Represented in both **figural** and **discursive** narratives, the site has occupied a borderline position between consciousness and unconsciousness. In the first extract, this position is indicated through Elaine's 'vision'; in the second extract, the unconscious is dominant in the painted image of the ravine together with its charged emblematic associations; in the third extract the landscape initially returns to the borderline region of the first extract before being delivered back into conscious territory. The ravine emerges as a place of psychic 'vision', of healing and, above all, of survival.

PART FIVE

BACKGROUND

MARGARET ATWOOD'S LIFE & WORK

Margaret Atwood is the highest profile writer ever to have emerged from Canada. Her novels and collections of poetry have been translated into over twenty languages, and her work is appreciated worldwide.

Born in Ottowa in 1939, Margaret Atwood spent a nomadic early childhood moving around the wilderness spaces of Northern Canada; her father was an entomologist and his young family accompanied him on research field-trips. In 1946, the family settled in Toronto, where Margaret Atwood attended high school and later university. She graduated in 1961 and in the same year published her first book, *Double Persephone*, a collection of poems. In the same year, she embarked upon postgraduate studies at Radcliffe College, Harvard University in the USA. Though she was already spending a great deal of time writing fiction and poetry, she was also researching her doctoral thesis on English Gothic fiction. This work was never completed as other priorities began to take over. By 1965, Margaret Atwood was becoming a well-established writer, particularly in Canada where a renaissance in Canadian writing had accompanied an upsurge in nationalist feeling.

Married to novelist Graeme Gibson, Margaret Atwood has remained based in Canada since her return from Harvard, though she has also spent periods living and working in Australia, Berlin, Edinburgh, New York, London, France and Ireland. She continues to travel widely giving readings and lectures. As well as being a prolific writer, she is also strongly committed to her work for Amnesty International, the Writer's Union of Canada (of which she was President in 1981–2), and to other cultural, political and environmental causes including PEN and Greenpeace.

LITERARY WORKS

Following the success of *Double Persephone* in 1961, Margaret Atwood published a second collection of poems: *The Circle Game* (1965) was awarded the Governor-General's Award, Canada's major literary prize, and this constituted an enormous achievement for so young a writer. Established as a poet, Atwood published her first novel in 1969: *The Edible Woman* had actually been written years earlier, but publication had been delayed because the manuscript had been lost by the publisher. *The Edible Woman* was a clearly 'political' novel in that it intersected with several issues raised by second-wave **feminism**.

The 1970s was a period of intense literary activity for Margaret Atwood. During the decade she published three novels: *Surfacing* (1972); *Lady Oracle* (1976) and *Life Before Man* (1977). She also published five books of poetry: *The Journals of Susanna Moodie* (1970), *Procedures for Underground* (1970), *Power Politics* (1971), *You are Happy* (1974) and *Two-Headed Poems* (1978). Her literary flexibility became apparent during this period: in 1972 she published *Survival: A Thematic Guide to Canadian Literature*, a children's book, *Up in the Tree* appeared in 1978, and in 1979, she published *Dancing Girls*, a collection of short stories. As such, Margaret Atwood showed exceptional versatility in writing in literary forms including academic criticism, poetry, novels, short stories and children's literature.

Margaret Atwood proved equally productive and versatile in the 1980s and 1990s, generally producing at least one major new book a year. In 1981, she published *True Stories* (poetry) and *Bodily Harm* (novel); in 1982, *Second Words: Selected Critical Prose*; in 1983, *Murder in the Dark* (prose poems), and *Bluebeard's Egg* (short stories); in 1984, *Interlunar* (poems); in 1985, *The Handmaid's Tale* (novel); in 1986, *Selected Poems II*; in 1987, *The Can Lit Food Book*; in 1988, *Cat's Eye* (novel); in 1990, *Margaret Atwood: Conversations* (edited interviews with the writer); in 1991, *Wilderness Tips* (short stories); in 1992, *Good Bones* (short fictions); in 1993, *The Robber Bride* (novel); in 1995, *Morning in the Burned House* (poetry), and *Strange Things: The Malevolent North in Canadian Literature* (criticism); in 1996, *Alias Grace* (novel); in 1998, *Eating Fire: Selected Poetry, 1965–1995*. Margaret Atwood has also edited *The Oxford Book of Canadian Verse in English* (1986), and co-edited *The Oxford Book of Short Stories in English* (1986) and *The New Oxford Book of Canadian Short Stories in English* (1995). There seems to be no literary format in which Atwood does not excel.

In terms of **genre**, Margaret Atwood's range is remarkable. Her novels have experimented with literary styles including **Gothic** romance (*Lady Oracle*), **dystopian** science-fiction (*The Handmaid's Tale*), and the spy-thriller form (*Bodily Harm*). Usually, several genres and styles are fused together within the one work; as a result, traces of **fictive autobiography** may blend with social documentary and fairy-tale or Gothic elements, as in *Cat's Eye*. Always, the poet's sense of rhythm, imagery and **metaphor** is evident: always, a 'political' impulse is clear. These 'politics' involve a concern with a range of socio-cultural issues including nationalism (particularly, but not exclusively, Canadian Nationalism), gender and environmentalism. Such 'political' currents suggest a concern for human rights issues rather than for ideological standpoints. For Atwood, 'politics' is a wide-ranging term indicating the way in which 'people relate to a power structure and vice-versa' (*Conversations*, p. 185). Margaret Atwood investigates this territory through her writing in the spirit of social reportage. She reflects 'political' situations as she sees them, but insists: 'I have to keep saying I'm a fiction writer [...] I'm not a propagandist' (*Conversations*, p. 30).

Atwood's concern for 'political' issues is clearly discernible in *Cat's Eye* where gender and inter-gender relationships are centralised. In addition, the novel also demonstrates Atwood's intellectual dexterity as she combines the theoretical **discourses** of art criticism and quantum mechanics within her story. Such dexterity is also manifested in Atwood's other works where fields as esoteric as military history and palaeontology are centralised within texts that make regular reference to an entire history of world literature. Generically versatile, hugely productive, academically dazzling, Margaret Atwood's writing continues to grip her international readership and to impress the critical establishment.

Historical background

Cat's Eye contains strong elements of social documentary in its historical journey through postwar Toronto, and in its 'eye-witness' account of a multicultural Toronto at the end of the 1980s. The novel as a whole connects with mounting concerns evident in Canada at the time of its publication relating to the extent, and long-term consequences, of

American encroachment into the Canadian socio-culture. A sense of growing 'internationalism' is apparent here, and this is regarded in both a positive and a negative light. In addition, issues of international terrorism, warfare and human rights offences are included in the novel, as is an emphasis upon a range of environmental anxieties. In Elaine's father's diatribes, the chaos of a ruined planet is outlined, and his predictions become increasingly accurate at the years roll by.

Intellectually, *Cat's Eye* connects with work in the field of theoretical physics, popularised in particular by Professor Stephen Hawking in the late 1980s. Hawking's book, *A Brief History of Time: From the Big Bang to Black Holes* (1988), became a worldwide best-seller. Several of the ideas of 'the new cosmology', promoted by Hawking and other scientists, entered into public consciousness and are appropriated by Atwood here.

These social, historical and intellectual contexts, together with the booming image of a 'world class' Toronto, create the feel of time and place in *Cat's Eye*. In addition, the novelist's stress on terrorism and on various refugee groups suggests a world in turmoil and disarray. This can be linked with North America's growing belligerence during the 1980s, particularly evident in its military interventions in the Middle East. Successive right-wing administrations in the USA (led by Ronald Reagan and George Bush) created a climate in which the arms trade flourished; this is directly condemned within *Cat's Eye* when Elaine notes that 'killing is endless now, it's an industry, there's money in it, and the good side and the bad side are pretty hard to tell apart' (p. 314).

In the USA, Canada and Europe at this time, prolonged economic boom led to a culture of conspicuous consumption which promoted self-interest and diminished social concern. Anxieties surrounding this mentality are evident in Elaine Risley's suspicion of the fashionable shops and buildings of Toronto which are inflected by American values, and in her dealings with the homeless and displaced victims of such a culture. An anticorporate outlook emerges as a result, as the greed and 'show' of 1980s society is both **satirised** and undermined.

In terms of the novel's social-documentary emphases, its oppositional 'political' stance and its intellectual activity, *Cat's Eye* captures the mood of contemporary Toronto as well as the postwar evolution of a socio-culture. Atwood asserts that she sees the novel as 'a vehicle for looking at society' *(Conversations*, p. 246), and *Cat's Eye* accords with this function in that its use of political movements (including 'second wave' **feminism**), fashions, and socio-cultural markers (for example, popular music and the 'beatnik' generation) are used to register a sense of Canadian society 'then' and 'now'. However, *Cat's Eye* is primarily the story of an individual's struggle with the power-games of interpersonal relationships and with the subsequent negotiation of a traumatised 'inner space'. As such, the political, cultural and socio-historical 'retrospective' elements of the novel are more of a contextualising background than the crux of the story itself.

LITERARY BACKGROUND

Margaret Atwood is extremely widely read and weaves allusions to a range of literary works into her novels and poetry. Usually, the **intertextuality** that results relies upon the Western literary canon, and Shakespeare is referred to or echoed particularly frequently. However, as in the Eduardo Galeano epigraph to the novel (see Summaries & Commentaries), writers from other cultures are also regularly alluded to in her work.

Shakespearean allusions in *Cat's Eye* are numerous. Atwood makes extensive use of *Macbeth* in the novel, while *Measure for Measure, King Lear* and *The Tempest* are also mentioned. The chain of references to *Macbeth* becomes overt at the beginning of Section V when Elaine notices tartan dresses in a Toronto department store. This triggers in Elaine a chain of associations which lead her to quote from *Macbeth*: '*My way of life*', she recalls, '*Is fall'n into the sere and yellow leaf*'. Elaine abandons the quote at this point, and the reader understands why she does so when the lines that proceed it are considered:

> 'And that which should accompany old age,
> As honour, love, obedience, troops of friends,
> I must not look to have; but, in their stead,
> Curses, not loud but deep ...' (Shakespeare, *Macbeth*, V.3.24–7)

These lines, which are too painful for Elaine to consider at this point in the narrative, should be intersected with Elaine's final words to the absent Cordelia as she flies towards her future at the end of the novel: 'This is what I miss, Cordelia: not something that's gone, but something that will never happen. Two old women giggling over their tea' (p. 421). Like Macbeth, Elaine understands that she cannot 'look to have' the comfort of friendship (in her case with Cordelia), in her 'old age'. The uncompleted quote from *Macbeth* therefore foreshadows Elaine's final sadness, and it does so barely a third of the way through the novel.

Other references to *Macbeth* litter the text: Cordelia performs in the play (dubbed 'The Tartans' by actors for superstitious reasons); Lady Macbeth is a figure used to describe the 'slippery deceitful smiles' of little girls (p. 113); Elaine's high school is called Burnham High, a name that consciously recalls the 'Birnam Wood' of Macbeth's final defeat. Given the information that *Macbeth* was on the Canadian school syllabus when Elaine was graduating from high school, references to this text are worked easily into the narrative (the young Elaine would, of course, be familiar with the play). These references are then used to suggest a range of more subtle meanings. The prevalence of quotes from and references to this play throughout *Cat's Eye* connect with supernatural imagery including that revolving round witches and ghosts; Cordelia, Grace and Carol are, for example, aligned with the three witches from *Macbeth*.

King Lear is a second Shakespearean text buried deep within *Cat's Eye*. The play is, in fact, referred to only once in the narrative, when the connotations of Cordelia's name are considered by Elaine (p. 263). However, in the repeated word 'nothing' which echoes through both *King Lear* and *Cat's Eye*, and in the images of the despotic father-figures of Lear and Cordelia's father, connections between the two texts are clearly announced. Further, both obsessively analyse the nature of identity, both weave connections between 'sight', 'insight' and 'blindness' (physical or **metaphorical**), and both operate through systems of 'doubles'. The subtle parallels between the two texts are not a matter of coincidence.

Measure for Measure becomes briefly centralised in Cordelia's role as a nun whose words are of crucial importance to Cordelia's characterisation in the novel (see p. 302). Similarly, *The Tempest* is briefly centralised in Cordelia's performance as an 'airy spirit', a role to which she could not be more suited (p. 303).

The Bible, another cornerstone of the Western canon, is also referred to regularly in this novel. The quote '*an eye for an eye*' (Exodus, 21:24) becomes particularly important given the network of metaphors and images relating to vision throughout *Cat's Eye*, and given the connections between 'sight' and 'insight' in particular ('An eye for an eye only leads to more blindness', p. 405). In addition, of course, the quotation connects with themes of 'justice' and vengeance in its justification for inhuman barbarity (Mrs Smeath's creed). Elaine's indoctrination at Sunday School also involves extensive Bible Studies and the gospels of Luke and St Paul, the Book of Corinthians, and several hymns and psalms are referenced in these sections. Further, religious iconography and imagery is also incorporated throughout.

In terms of style and plot, *Cat's Eye* develops intertextual relationships with a variety of other works. The **motif** of live burial, and the notion of an evil **doppelgänger** that has split off from a single personality, are **Gothic** impulses dominant in Edgar Allan Poe's 'The Fall of the House of Usher' (1839), and Henry James's *The Turn of the Screw* (1898), respectively. Elements from a variety of Gothic works can also be detected in the techniques, allusions and motifs of *Cat's Eye* (see Themes, on Gothic). Further, Margaret Atwood's childhood addiction to the frequently savage *Grimms' Fairy Tales* (European folk tales collected together at the beginning of the nineteenth century) is registered in the Grimm-like tale of the two sisters and the mirror (p. 211). It is also echoed in the emphasis upon metamorphosis and witchcraft as located at the heart of both *Grimms' Fairy Tales* and *Cat's Eye*.

The narrative strategies of this novel work through twinned **discourses** that involve theoretical physics and art criticism: the former is, as the second epigraph to the novel suggests, largely drawn from Stephen Hawking's *A Brief History of Time: From the Big Bang to Black Holes* (1988). References to this work and to the ideas that it contains are not direct, but form a basis for Stephen's discussions of space-time, dimensions, time-travel and so on. The discourse of art history and criticism is not drawn from any specific source, but appropriates several different elements of contemporary academic thought. Similarly, Atwood's treatment of second-wave **feminism** within the novel does not rely upon sourced material or to allusions to literary texts. The more ridiculous excesses of the feminist movement that are **satirised** in the novel (see pp. 378–9) are drawn from the movement's manifestation in the popular culture in the 1970s in particular, and are not derived from specific feminist writers.

Cat's Eye is, then, a highly intertextual novel that incorporates allusions to a wide variety of other literary works. Direct or indirect references to these works abound, while broader contexts of academic or political enquiry are drawn from a range of nonspecifiable works that have entered into the socio-cultural economy.

To understand and appreciate every allusion in *Cat's Eye* would be to enjoy as extensive a literary and cultural knowledge as the novelist herself, but to pursue as many allusions as possible does yield dividends. The allusions and references lead the reader to develop an understanding of less overt meanings within the text, and to forge connections between networks of imagery and discourses that would not become apparent otherwise (see Further Reading).

PART SIX

CRITICAL HISTORY & BROADER PERSPECTIVES

CONTEMPORARY VIEWS

Cat's Eye was nominated for the Booker Prize in 1989. Although the novel has proved less controversial than earlier works by Margaret Atwood (such as *The Edible Woman* and *The Handmaid's Tale*), it was debated by several **feminist** writers upon its publication because of its apparently anti-feminist attack upon female–female relationships. This reductive approach to the text was, though, quickly undermined in subsequent feminist analyses which have concentrated on the novelist's focus upon issues of gender and society in *Cat's Eye* (see Themes, on Gender).

In recent critical responses to the novel, critics have largely taken a **narratological** approach in concentrating upon the way in which Elaine 'writes' her story in **discursive** and **figural** versions (see Narrative Techniques). Other critics have taken a **generic** approach and have, for example, connected **Gothic** elements within the novel with a feminist discourse (see Themes, on Gothic). Other generic approaches have included exploring the novelist's use of the **fictive autobiography** form (see Reading *Cat's Eye*).

In addition, **intertextual** analyses of *Cat's Eye* have traced the novel's relationship with other texts, including Shakespearean drama and fairy-tales or myths (see Literary Background). Issues of perception and reality within the novel have also been extensively debated, particularly in relation to questions raised by Elaine Risley's distorted or unreliable vision (see Themes, on Vision).

Cat's Eye has therefore been discussed through analyses that respond largely to its 'inner space' narrative and to its intricate fusion of narrative strategies and theoretical **discourses**. Critical appraisals of *Cat's Eye* are continuing to be generated.

Margaret Atwood, *Conversations*, ed. Earl G. Ingersoll, Virago, 1992

An extremely useful collection of interviews with the novelist between 1972 and 1990. This text contains extensive biographical information about the novelist, and provides detail about Margaret Atwood's 'political' and literary positions. Widely available, this invaluable book should be regarded as essential reading by students of Margaret Atwood's poetry and fiction

Margaret Atwood, *Second Words: Selected Critical Prose*, Anansi, Toronto, 1982. Reprinted 1996

Contains a fascinating essay on 'Witches', and comment that expands understanding of a range of issues raised in Margaret Atwood's work

Coral Ann Howells, *Margaret Atwood*, Macmillan, 1996

See Chapter 8, 'Atwood's Retrospective Art: *Cat's Eye*', and Chapter 4, 'Atwoodian Gothic: From *Lady Oracle* to *The Robber Bride*' in particular. This accessible book is highly recommended to students

M.K. MacMurraugh-Kavanagh, '"Through a Glass Darkly": Fields of Vision, Identity and Metaphor in Margaret Atwood's *Cat's Eye* and Shakespeare's *King Lear*', *British Journal of Canadian Studies*, vol.12:1 (1997), pp. 78–91

This essay explores the connections between *King Lear* and *Cat's Eye*, and discusses the theme of 'vision' in both

Colin Nicholson, ed., *Margaret Atwood: Writing and Subjectivity*, Macmillan and St Martin's Press, 1994

This is an extremely useful collection of essays that should be consulted if possible: See in particular Chapter 9, 'Gender as Genre: Atwood's Autobiographical "I"', by Sherrill Grace. This discussion analyses the construction of the gendered subject in the autobiographical paintings that Elaine Risley produces, and in the autobiographical life-story presented in the **discursive** narrative

Eleonora Rao, *Strategies for Identity: The Fiction of Margaret Atwood*, Peter Lang Publishing, Inc., 1993 ['Writing About Women: Feminist Literary Studies' series]

See in particular Chapter 3, 'Cognitive Questions', which investigates the issues of perception and reality in *Cat's Eye*, and Chapter 4, 'Writing the Female Subject' which deals with the question of gender 'difference' in *Cat's Eye*. These are rigorous essays, but they are useful in developing sophisticated readings of the novel

Constance Rooke, *Fear of the Open Heart: Essays on Contemporary Canadian Writing*, Coach House Press, 1989
  Contains an excellent essay on Margaret Atwood's imagery

Kathryn Van Spanckeren and Jan Garden Castro, eds, *Margaret Atwood: Visions and Forms*, South Illinois University Press, Carbondale and Edwardsville, 1988
  Contains an illuminating interview with the novelist, and an interesting general introduction to the novelist's work

Sharon Rose Wilson, *Margaret Atwood's Fairy-Tale Politics*, University Press of Mississippi, Jackson, 1993
  See Chapter 11, '*Cat's Eye* Vision: "*Rapunzel*" and "*The Snow Queen*"'. This chapter draws **intertextual** parallels between a range of fairy-tale motifs and *Cat's Eye*. In this discussion it is suggested that Cordelia may be a victim of incestuous abuse

Loraine York, ed., *Various Atwoods: Essays on the later poems, short fiction, and novels*, Anansi, Toronto, 1995
  See Molly Hite, 'An Eye for an I: The Disciplinary Society in *Cat's Eye*', and Natalie Cooke, 'The Politics of Ventriloquism: Margaret Atwood's Fictive Confessions'. The former analyses the operation of the monitoring gaze upon women in a 'disciplinary' society, and the latter investigates the interaction between Atwood's fictional 'confessors' and the reader

Simone de Beauvoir, *The Second Sex* (1949, translated into English 1953), Pan Books, 1988 edition
  Useful for developing an understanding of 'second-wave' **feminism**

Stephen Hawking, *A Brief History of Time: From the Big Bang to Black Holes*, Bantam Books, 1988
  For further information about theories of 'space-time'

Victor Sage and Allan Lloyd Smith, eds, *Modern Gothic: A Reader*, Manchester University Press, 1996
  For further reading around the **Gothic genre**.

Bram Stoker, *Dracula* (1897), Penguin Classics, 1993 edition
  The classic vampire story which usefully intersects with the Eduardo Galeano epigraph to the novel

Y

Mary Shelley, *Frankenstein, or The Modern Prometheus* (1818), Penguin Books, 1985 edition
> The Gothic impulses in this text include the transgression of boundaries, and psychic energies springing from the unconscious. Excellent background reading for *Cat's Eye*

WORKS WHICH HAVE ECHOES IN CAT'S EYE

Henry James, *The Turn of the Screw* (1898), J.M. Dent, 1992 edition

Edgar Allan Poe, 'The Fall of the House of Usher' (1839), in *The Complete Tales and Poems of Edgar Allan Poe*, Penguin, 1982 edition)

The Brothers Grimm: The Complete Fairy Tales, Wordsworth, 1997 edition

The Bible, especially the Book of Exodus

William Shakespeare, *Macbeth, Measure for Measure, King Lear, The Tempest*: all Arden Shakespeare

World events	Author's life	Other literary works
1867 British North America Act establishes Dominion of Canada		
1894 X-rays discovered		
1914 Outbreak of First World War		
1915 Einstein postulates general theory of relativity		
1918 Max Planck wins Nobel Prize for Quantum Theory		
1930 Planet Pluto discovered		
1933 Hitler becomes German Chancellor		
1939 Outbreak of Second World War	**1939** Margaret Atwood born, Ottawa	
	early 1940s Lives in rural Ontario where father is entomologist, and Quebec	
1942 Enrico Fermi splits atom		
1945 War ends; atomic bombs dropped on Hiroshima and Nagasaki		
	1946 Settles in Toronto where father becomes university professor	
		1949 George Orwell, *Nineteen Eighty-four;* Simone de Beauvoir, *Le Deuxième Sexe – The Second Sex*
1953 Coronation of Elizabeth II		
1954 Elizabeth II and Duke of Edinburgh begin extensive Commonwealth tour		
1958 US launches first moon rocket (unsuccessful); NASA established		
1961 Yuri Gagarin makes first manned space flight	**1961** Graduates; first poems, *Double Persephone;* goes to Harvard to study American literature	**1961** Iris Murdoch, *A Severed Head;* Muriel Spark, *The Prime of Miss Jean Brodie*
		1962 Rachel Carson, *Silent Spring;* Doris Lessing, *The Golden Notebook*

World events	Author's life	Other literary works
1963 First 'Pop Art' exhibition, New York; 'second wave' feminist movement becoming organised in North America		**1963** Mary McCarthy, *The Group;* Betty Friedan, *The Feminine Mystique*
	1965 *The Circle Game* (poems) awarded Governor General's Award	
1966 Mini skirts become fashionable		
	1967 Marries James Polk	
1968 Pierre Trudeau becomes Prime Minister of Canada		**1968** Alexander Solzhenitsyn, *Cancer Ward;* Marguerite Yourcenar, *L'Oeuvre au noir – The Abyss*
1969 Apollo moon landing; first men on the moon	**1969** *The Edible Woman* (novel)	
1970 2 million die in Biafran civil war	**1970-8** Five further books of poetry	**1970** Michel Tournier, *The Erl King*
1971 Greenpeace founded to protest about nuclear testing in Alaska		**1971** Germaine Greer, *The Female Eunuch*
1972 US Congress endorses Equal Rights Amendment	**1972** *Survival,* controversial study of Canadian literature; *Surfacing* (novel)	
1973 Abortion legalised in USA; Arab-Israeli War; Middle East oil embargoes placed on USA	**1973** Divorced; lives with partner Graeme Gibson, novelist	
		1974 Ursula Le Guin, *The Dispossessed*
1975 War ends in Vietnam		**1975** Joanna Russ, *The Female Man*
	1976 Daughter Jess born; *Lady Oracle* (novel)	**1976** Marge Piercy, *Woman on the Edge of Time*
1977 French adopted as official language in Quebec	**1977** *Life before Man* (novel)	
1978 World's population *c.*4.4 billion, increasing by approx. 200,000 per day		
1979 Shah of Iran exiled; women protest against Islamic fundamentalist strictures: 'Freedom, not the chador'	**1979** *Dancing Girls* (short stories)	**1979** Gabrielle Roy, *Children of My Heart*

World events	Author's life	Other literary works
1980 Iran-Iraq war; Ronald Reagan becomes president of USA		
1980-9 Half the world's tropical rainforests destroyed		
	1981 Made President of Writers Union of Canada; *True Stories* (short stories); *Bodily Harm* (novel)	**1981** Salman Rushdie, *Midnight's Children;* Alice Walker, *The Color Purple*
1982 Canada's Constitution Act severs last legal links with UK; Canada protests at damage done to its forests by acid rain	**1982** *Second Words: Selected Critical Prose*	**1982** Alice Munro, *Lives of Girls and Women*
	1983-4 *Murder in the Dark* (poems), *Interlunar* (poems) and *Bluebeard's Egg* (short stories)	
		1984 J.G. Ballard, *Empire of the Sun*
1985 Hole in ozone layer over North Pole discovered	**1985** *The Handmaid's Tale* (novel)	**1985** Angela Carter, *Nights at the Circus;* Patrick Suskind, *Perfume*
1986 World's worst nuclear power disaster at Chernobyl in Ukraine		
		1987 Kazuo Ishiguro, *An Artist of the Floating World;* Toni Morrison, *Beloved*
1988 George Bush becomes president of USA	**1988** *Cat's Eye*	**1988** Stephen Hawking, *A Brief History of Time;* Thomas Harris, *The Silence of the Lambs*
1990 Anti-feminist backlash; Iraqi invasion of Kuwait leads to Gulf War		
1991 Up to 20 million Africans dependent on emergency food aid	**1991-2** *Wilderness Tips* (short stories), *Good Bones* (short fictions)	
	1993 *The Robber Bride* (novel)	
1995 Quebec narrowly votes against independence	**1995** *Strange Things: The Malevolent North in Canadian Literature*	
	1996 *Alias Grace* (novel)	

allegory a story, image or representation presented in such a way as to have more than one identifiable meaning

discourse traditionally, conversation, or a serious discussion or examination of a learned topic

discursive from discourse, a verbal narrative based on discussion or exposition

doppelgänger (German, literally 'double-goer') a ghostly double of a human person, an apparition, a wraith; see also double

double an *alter ego* who bears an uncanny partial resemblance to the self and reveals aspects of the self which have been repressed; as such, the 'double' is both familiar and sinister

dystopia anti-utopia, the opposite of utopia: invented futuristic nightmare world based on current social, political and economic trends and warning against their possible disastrous implications

epigraph quotations usually found at the beginning of a book, or chapter of a book

existentialism a philosophical position which maintains that the universe is an inexplicable, meaningless and dangerous environment where the individual encounters only futility and ultimate nothingness; it is associated with postwar European intellectual activity and, in North America, with the beatnik generation

feminism referring to the numerous different approaches involved in investigating the subordination of women in patriarchal society (i.e. man-centred society based upon 'the law of the father')

fictive autobiography the life-story of a fictional character

figural an allegorical mode of representation in which written or painted images carry hidden meanings and connections

genre, generic a type of literature, e.g. Gothic romance, spy-thriller, or detective novel

Gothic see Themes, on Gothic

idiomatic a phrase or way of expressing something in popular language, e.g. 'making a spectacle of yourself'

intertextuality refers to the many and various kinds of relationships that exist between texts; can be used to indicate direct or indirect echoes from other texts or literary genres

irony saying one thing to mean another; using words to convey the opposite of their literal meaning; saying something that has one meaning for someone knowledgable about a situation and another meaning for those who are not

Künstlerroman from the German, meaning 'artist-novel'; novel which traces the development of an artist or writer

malapropism a comic verbal confusion

metaphor figure of speech in which a descriptive term, or name, or action characteristic of one object is applied to another to suggest a likeness between them, but which does not use 'like' or 'as' in the comparison

motif a recurrent element which is significant in the overall structure of meaning in the text

narratology the study and theory of the ways a story can be told

paradox a statement that seems self-contradicatory; something which may seem absurd or unbelievable, yet which may be true

parody a humorous or ludicrous imitation of a piece of serious writing or speech; it is affectionate humour in the style of that which is being parodied

satire literature that explores vice or folly and makes them appear ridiculous; usually condemnatory in intent

symbol something that by association in thought comes to represent something else; often an object that represents something abstract

AUTHOR OF THIS NOTE

Madeleine MacMurraugh-Kavanagh was educated at the University of Reading where she is now a lecturer in English Literature. She has published widely in the fields of modern drama, media studies, and feminist writing.

NOTES

York Notes Advanced (£3.99 each)

Margaret Atwood
Cat's Eye

Margaret Atwood
The Handmaid's Tale

Jane Austen
Mansfield Park

Jane Austen
Persuasion

Jane Austen
Pride and Prejudice

Alan Bennett
Talking Heads

William Blake
Songs of Innocence and of Experience

Charlotte Brontë
Jane Eyre

Emily Brontë
Wuthering Heights

Angela Carter
Nights at the Circus

Geoffrey Chaucer
The Franklin's Tale

Geoffrey Chaucer
The Miller's Prologue and Tales

Geoffrey Chaucer
Prologue To the Canterbury Tales

Geoffrey Chaucer
The Wife of Bath's Prologue and Tale

Joseph Conrad
Heart of Darkness

Charles Dickens
Great Expectations

Charles Dickens
Hard Times

Emily Dickinson
Selected Poems

John Donne
Selected Poems

Carol Ann Duffy
Selected Poems

George Eliot
Middlemarch

George Eliot
The Mill on the Floss

T.S. Eliot
Selected Poems

F. Scott Fitzgerald
The Great Gatsby

E.M. Forster
A Passage to India

Brian Friel
Translations

Thomas Hardy
The Mayor of Casterbridge

Thomas Hardy
The Return of the Native

Thomas Hardy
Selected Poems

Thomas Hardy
Tess of the d'Urbervilles

Seamus Heaney
Selected Poems from Opened Ground

Nathaniel Hawthorne
The Scarlet Letter

Kazou Ishiguru
The Remains of the Day

James Joyce
Dubliners

John Keats
Selected Poems

Christopher Marlowe
Doctor Faustus

Arthur Miller
Death of a Salesman

John Milton
Paradise Lost Books I & II

Toni Morrison
Beloved

William Shakespeare
Antony and Cleopatra

William Shakespeare
As You Like It

William Shakespeare
Hamlet

William Shakespeare
King Lear

William Shakespeare
Measure for Measure

William Shakespeare
The Merchant of Venice

William Shakespeare
A Midsummer Night's Dream

William Shakespeare
Much Ado About Nothing

William Shakespeare
Othello

William Shakespeare
Richard II

William Shakespeare
Romeo and Juliet

William Shakespeare
The Taming of the Shrew

William Shakespeare
The Tempest

William Shakespeare
The Winter's Tale

George Bernard Shaw
Saint Joan

Mary Shelley
Frankenstein

Alice Walker
The Color Purple

Oscar Wilde
The Importance of Being Earnest

Tennessee Williams
A Streetcar Named Desire

John Webster
The Duchess of Malfi

Virginia Woolf
To the Lighthouse

W.B. Yeats
Selected Poems

OTHER TITLES

GCSE and equivalent levels (£3.50 each)

Maya Angelou
I Know Why the Caged Bird Sings

Jane Austen
Pride and Prejudice

Alan Ayckbourn
Absent Friends

Elizabeth Barrett Browning
Selected Poems

Robert Bolt
A Man for All Seasons

Harold Brighouse
Hobson's Choice

Charlotte Brontë
Jane Eyre

Emily Brontë
Wuthering Heights

Shelagh Delaney
A Taste of Honey

Charles Dickens
David Copperfield

Charles Dickens
Great Expectations

Charles Dickens
Hard Times

Charles Dickens
Oliver Twist

Roddy Doyle
Paddy Clarke Ha Ha Ha

George Eliot
Silas Marner

George Eliot
The Mill on the Floss

William Golding
Lord of the Flies

Oliver Goldsmith
She Stoops To Conquer

Willis Hall
The Long and the Short and the Tall

Thomas Hardy
Far from the Madding Crowd

Thomas Hardy
The Mayor of Casterbridge

Thomas Hardy
Tess of the d'Urbervilles

Thomas Hardy
The Withered Arm and other Wessex Tales

L.P. Hartley
The Go-Between

Seamus Heaney
Selected Poems

Susan Hill
I'm the King of the Castle

Barry Hines
A Kestrel for a Knave

Louise Lawrence
Children of the Dust

Harper Lee
To Kill a Mockingbird

Laurie Lee
Cider with Rosie

Arthur Miller
The Crucible

Arthur Miller
A View from the Bridge

Robert O'Brien
Z for Zachariah

Frank O'Connor
My Oedipus Complex and other stories

George Orwell
Animal Farm

J.B. Priestley
An Inspector Calls

Willy Russell
Educating Rita

Willy Russell
Our Day Out

J.D. Salinger
The Catcher in the Rye

William Shakespeare
Henry IV Part 1

William Shakespeare
Henry V

William Shakespeare
Julius Caesar

William Shakespeare
Macbeth

William Shakespeare
The Merchant of Venice

William Shakespeare
A Midsummer Night's Dream

William Shakespeare
Much Ado About Nothing

William Shakespeare
Romeo and Juliet

William Shakespeare
The Tempest

William Shakespeare
Twelfth Night

George Bernard Shaw
Pygmalion

Mary Shelley
Frankenstein

R.C. Sherriff
Journey's End

Rukshana Smith
Salt on the snow

John Steinbeck
Of Mice and Men

Robert Louis Stevenson
Dr Jekyll and Mr Hyde

Jonathan Swift
Gulliver's Travels

Robert Swindells
Daz 4 Zoe

Mildred D. Taylor
Roll of Thunder, Hear My Cry

Mark Twain
Huckleberry Finn

James Watson
Talking in Whispers

William Wordsworth
Selected Poems

A Choice of Poets

Mystery Stories of the Nineteenth Century including The Signalman

Nineteenth Century Short Stories

Poetry of the First World War

Six Women Poets